Bluegill

Fly Fishing & Flies

Terry & Roxanne Wilson

FOREWORD BY DAVE WHITLOCK
ILLUSTRATED BY LEFTY WILSON

Frank Amato PORTLAND

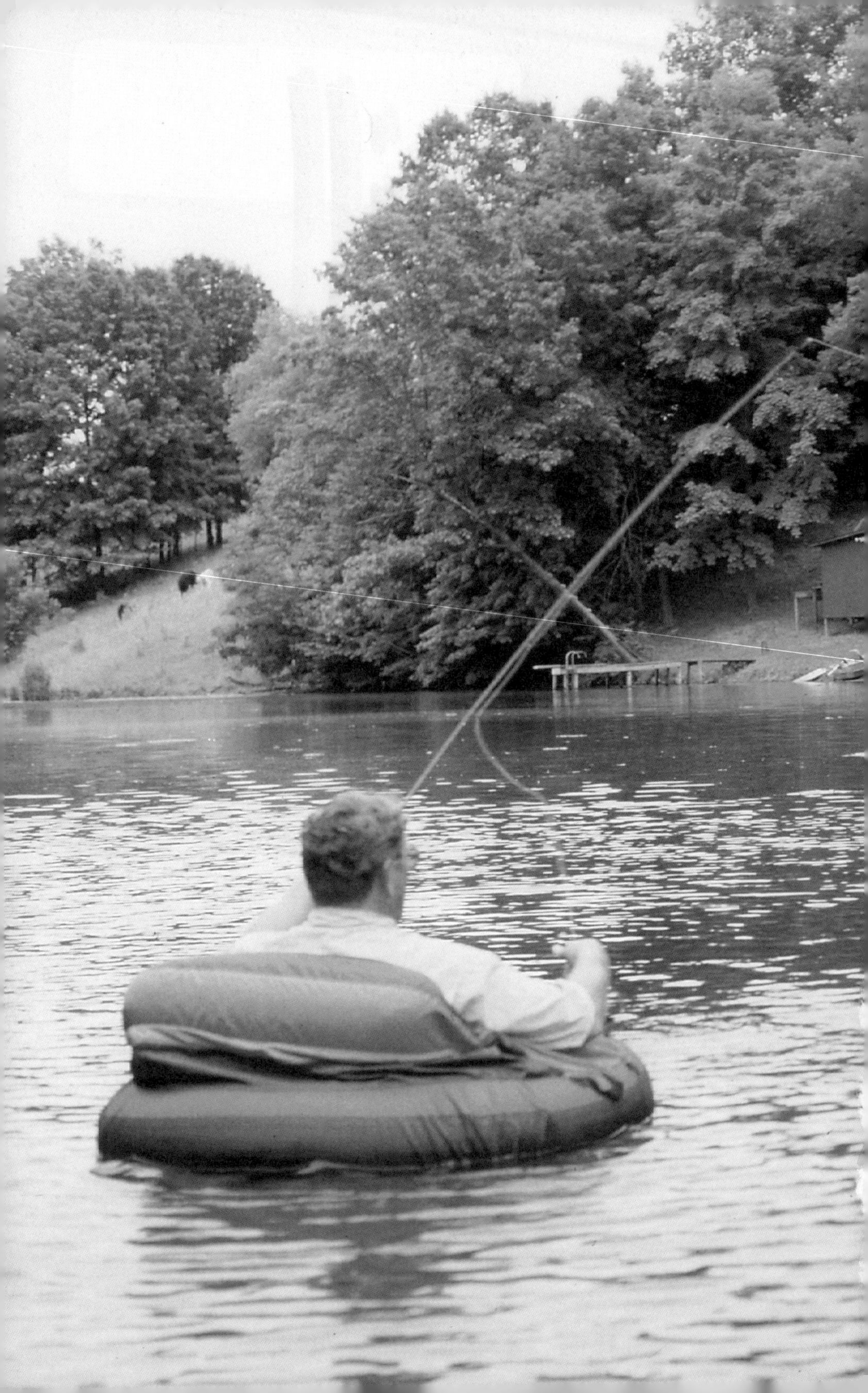

Bluegill
Fly Fishing & Flies

Terry & Roxanne Wilson

FOREWORD BY DAVE WHITLOCK
ILLUSTRATED BY LEFTY WILSON

Frank Amato PORTLAND

Dedication

To our parents for nurturing our love of fishing and our children and grandchildren who tolerate the obsession it has become.

TERRY AND ROXANNE WILSON are Illinois flatlanders by birth transplanted into the lakes region of southwest Missouri's Ozark Mountains by choice. Together they have accumulated seventy-five years of bluegill wisdom. Their warmwater fly-fishing obsession has translated into promoting catch-and-release fly fishing through writing, speaking, and teaching. For more than a decade they have presented innovative, practical fly-fishing methods for bass, bluegill, crappie, gar, and channel catfish in *Warmwater Fly Fishing, FIy Fishing Quarterly, Bassmaster, Ontario Out of Doors, Thicket's Hunting and Fishing Journal, The Fishing and Hunting Journal, Popular Flyfishing, The Flyfisher,* and other magazines.

Terry and Roxanne are members of the Smallmouth Alliance and are active life members of the Federation of Fly Fishers. They were presented with the Don Harger Memorial Award in 1996 for their contributions to the sport of fly fishing.

Terry began writing in 1981 with humorous tales for *Ducks Unlimited* followed by a sentimental story about hunting with his grandfather published in *Quail Unlimited.* Terry's storytelling skills have been honed in the classroom as a history teacher for thirty-four years.

Roxanne's fascination with fly fishing began with a borrowed rod. Eventually it was reclaimed, but memories of summer evenings with willing bluegill remained. She has since enjoyed exploring lakes, ponds, and streams with her fly rod and camera.

Bluegill Fly Fishing and Flies is their first book.

Acknowledgments

We've been exceedingly fortunate to have crossed paths with many knowledgeable and nurturing people who have contributed mightily toward transforming our addiction to bluegill fly fishing into the pages of this book. We are forever indebted to these good folks:

Chuck Tryon, whose counsel and advice we have continually sought and who, fortunately, couldn't say "no." For his encouragement, his insistence on numerous rewrites, for his editing skills, and mostly for his friendship.

John "Lefty" Wilson, whose illustrations so beautifully supplement our written words and who first encouraged us to write.

Mike Kruse, for sharing so generously his immense knowledge about our beloved bluegill and for guiding us to the right professional sources.

Don Niccum and Doug Farthing for using their considerable abilities at the tying vise to create the flies used in the photographs in Chapter 4.

Bob and Sue Ann Duvendack, who regularly share their piece of "bluegill heaven" and whose friendship has enriched our lives.

Fred Stevenson, who has encouraged our warmwater endeavors for over a decade, for sharing his knowledge as well as his wealth of nationwide contacts.

David Halblom, whose generosity with time and knowledge is without limits.

Leon Chandler, who willingly shared his international experiences and singular expertise.

Dennis Galyardt for encouragement and bluegill fly patterns.

Lew Vogele, Jon Cave, Ron Kruger, and Danny Cline for invaluable information about regional bluegill fishing.

Tom Yocom, Tony Accardo, Carl Crapse and the late C.B. Nance for sharing their extensive knowledge about bluegill flies and equipment and finally, to all of the pond, lake, and streamside philosophers who shared their experiences, their flies, and in the process enriched our experiences and broadened our knowledge.

© 1999 Terry & Roxanne Wilson

ALL RIGHTS RESERVED. No part of this book may be reproduced in any means without the written consent of the Publisher, except in the case of brief excerpts in critical reviews and articles.

Published in 1999 by:
Frank Amato Publications, Inc.
PO Box 82112
Portland, Oregon 97282
(503) 653-8108

Softbound UPC: 0-66066-00378-2
Softbound ISBN: 1-57188-176-X

All photographs taken by the authors unless otherwise noted.
Cover Photo: Roxanne Wilson
Illustrations: Lefty Wilson

Book Design: Tony Amato

Printed in Canada

10 9 8 7 6 5 4 3 2

Contents

Foreword . . . 8

Introduction . . . 11

Chapter 1:
> **BEAUTIFUL VIBRATIONS** 12

Chapter 2:
> **GEARING UP** 23

Chapter 3:
> **BULLY'S BLUEGILL SPIDER** 36

Chapter 4:
> **COMPLETING THE FLY BOX** 43

Chapter 5:
> **CHOOSING THE RIGHT WATER** 73

Chapter 6:
> **THE BLUEGILL'S SPRING** 91

Chapter 7:
> **THE BLUEGILL'S SUMMER** 101

Chapter 8:
> **AS THE WATER COOLS** 112

Chapter 9:
> **EFFECTIVE PRESENTATIONS** 121

Chapter 10:
> **PUTTING THE PIECES TOGETHER** 139

Bibliography . . . 150

Index . . . 150

Foreword

by Dave Whitlock

The bluegill has been first with me for as long as I can remember. The first fish I ever caught was a three-and-one-half-inch bluegill. The first fish I caught on both a lure and a fly were bluegill. The first fish I caught on a back cast at age 9 was a bluegill. The first fish I caught on a fly I tied was a bluegill. The first fish my sons Joel and Alan caught were bluegills. When Sage's rod designer Jerry Siem traveled to Arkansas to have me help him test Sage's revolutionary SPL 1- and 0-weight rods, he asked that he and I first test the big bluegills in my pond. And the first fish most of our fly fishing students catch are bluegills.

I remember more vividly the first 12-inch bluegill I caught on a fly than the first 12-pound brown trout or 12-pound largemouth bass. Why? Well it's like this, for me a bluegill that size on a fly was much more difficult to come by because it took me 34 years, while the big brown only took 23 years and the big bass 28 years.

I was in New Hampshire, of all places, exploring a remote bass pond that proved to have a huge population of little bass, mostly one quarter to one and one half pounds. Almost every cast with any popper, diver, or streamer got a strike. But, three times I hooked unseen fish that were so brutishly strong and quick that each promptly pulled my leader into the thick cover and broke the 2X leader tip. I knew there were only supposed to be bass, some small chubs, and yellow perch in the pond. Puzzled, I tied on a 0X tippet and another fly. Several casts later, I hooked another mystery monster. It took me in and out of the shoreline, around dead falls and lilies, then actually pulled the canoe out into deep water, while peeling yards of line after it. Once, twice, three times the demon lunged away. Then finally it reluctantly allowed me to bring it near the surface alongside the canoe. Out of the dark, reddish-brown stained water came a hubcap-size form. I almost fainted when I saw it and recognized it as a giant, orange-breasted, male bluegill. Its black ear flap was as big as a quarter. It was almost too big to believe! It was larger than a plate, simply an awesome sight to behold. I landed two more of these trophies before the day ended. The pond had been stocked with bluegill which apparently had not reproduced much and had just steadily grown into these monsters.

I'm fortunate in my work to have known a lot of wonderful waters where big bass and trout can be had fly fishing. But I can count on less than ten fingers places where I know trophy bluegill can be found. Most of these I had to swear in blood not to reveal to receive permission to fish.

Big bluegills are not only rare, they are also as selective as any trout, maybe even more so. I was enlightened to this fact about 15 years ago with a most memorable experience. It happened like the New Hampshire incident, when I least expected it. I had an opportunity to consult for a prominent St. Louis architect, George Helmuth, on his 2000-acre Missouri fish and game habitat. During a visit he asked me to check his spring lake, which was a magnificent man-made pond that had two huge, gushing, limestone springs on either end of the pond. It was stocked with big rainbows, but some good-sized native bass, chain pickerel, and panfish could also be seen around the perimeter of the turquoise-clear pond.

I focused on catching the arm-long rainbows that cruised the shorelines and channels, but most of my casts spooked them, or I thought so until I realized that it was the big dinner-plate size bluegill that I spooked as I cast and then they would in turn scare the trout. I was finally cautious enough to take a few of the big bluegills and quite a few trout by hiding, making a long cast with a 12-foot, 6X leader and allowing my scud fly to sink into the vegetation. Then I'd just wait until a big gill would cruise by, move the scud and it would swim down and carefully (oh so carefully) suck up my scud fly. Only one in about six bluegills would take. The trout were much more gullible and nearly every one that saw the scud would quickly gobble it.

Another interesting thing about this experience was that I lost a higher percentage of the big bluegill than the trout. The trout easily weighed two or three times more, but the big bluegills made such strong, long, hard dashes into cover that I couldn't begin to stop them on the 5X tippet that I had to use to get them to take my fly. I gained a whole new respect for bluegill selectivity and fighting power that day.

I doubt if there's any argument among freshwater fishermen, particularly those that fly fish, that bluegills are one of our most significantly popular game fish. This is especially true if you consider how many of us discovered how much fun fishing could be by catching our first bluegill. Certainly they are at their best when stalked, cast to, hooked, and fought on *fly tackle*.

Fly rods made of super-sensitive graphite, especially those made to cast 4-, 3-, 2-, 1-, and 0-weight line, and the wonderful ultra-strong leader materials available now allow us to reach a special plateau of angling for them and, therefore, finally allowing them the respect and stature they so deserve.

When I hear, read, or see anything about catching big bluegill, it immediately gets my undivided attention. That's exactly what happened when Terry and Roxanne Wilson told me of their plans to publish a book titled *Bluegill Fly Fishing & Flies*. They sent me a rough copy to read and write a Foreword for. Once I began reading it, I couldn't stop until I'd read all ten chapters. Every chapter is loaded with excellent motivation and instruction about fly fishing for big bluegill wherever they swim, all year long.

You'll be impressed by their dedication and knowledge of the *great big, little fish*. This makes me wonder why such a special book took so long to be written which finally, perfectly describes the sensation we all feel when we hook a big bluegill on a fly rod. In Buddy's words, "Love them beautiful vibrations."

Introduction

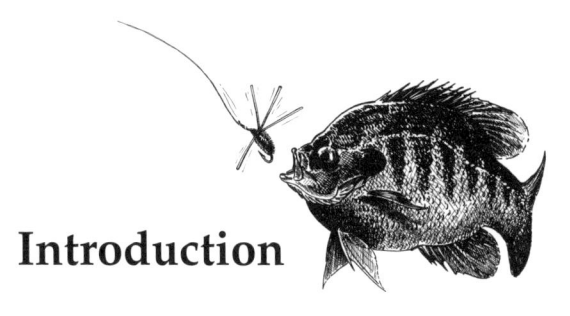

Big bluegills have provided us with more than four decades of angling thrills. We're not after the little guys that dart around at the shallow edges of the pond, but the ones that a man can't get his fingers around, the ones Southerners call "hubcaps" for their heft and girth. The more of these brutes we can catch, the better.

Why bluegill? They are available to fishermen in nearly every state in the Union, their pugnacity is legendary, and their tenacious yanking, diving, twisting battles are unforgettable. They're fun, anywhere and just about any time.

Many fishermen will tell you bluegill fishing is "too easy," they "don't fish for them after the spawn" and, "they're great for kids." Nothing to be taken seriously. After all, in the minds of most anglers game fish are symbols of strength and skill. Catching big bluegills is usually a footnote to their fish stories.

The truth is that large bluegills can be as selective as any trout. Catching them, whether in California, New York, or Missouri, is demanding and challenging sport. They shouldn't be dismissed as "too easy" because they are the lucky and smart survivors of a thousand attempts by their cousins to annihilate them. The fish we're after are careful about what they eat and where they eat it. Finding and catching them after the spawn have baffled many a self-proclaimed angling expert who ignored the necessity of learning about the species and its unique habits.

Catching big bluegills shouldn't come to an end when the spawn is finished. For decades, we've fished year-round for bluegills, we've talked with countless other bluegill lovers and compiled this information and good advice. The following pages are not accounts of all the good times we had. It's a report of what we learned so that our readers can share our joy in this challenging sport.

Whether you're a sometimes fly-fisher, a veteran fly-caster who has chased other species, or a practicing bluegill fanatic, come join us at the water's edge for a lifetime of pure delight.

Chapter 1
BEAUTIFUL VIBRATIONS

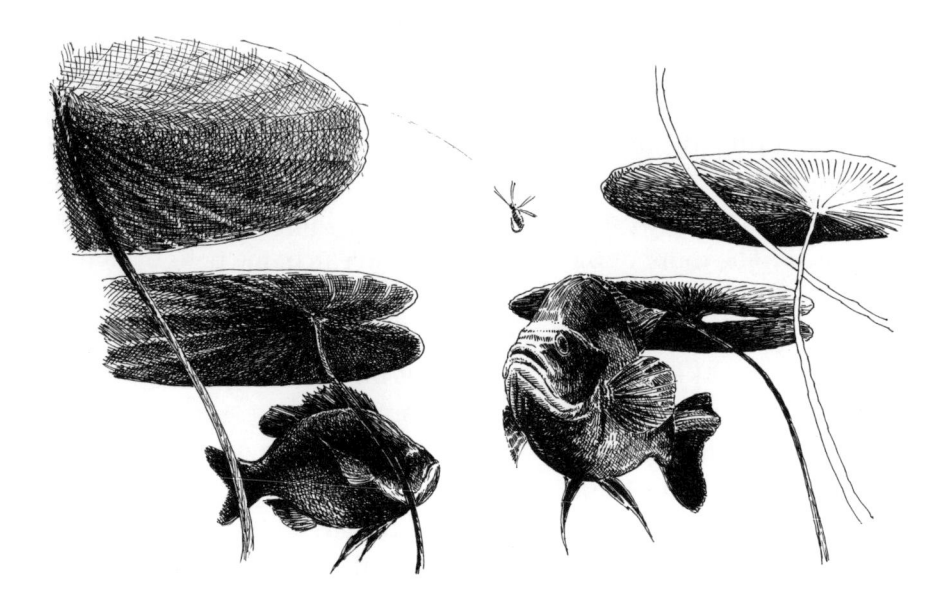

"OUNCE FOR POUND, THE BLUEGILL IS THE FIGHTINGEST FISH IN THE POND."

Fred Stevenson
Bluegill author and lecturer
Huntsville, Alabama, 1996

Bluegills provide more people with angling thrills than any fish that swims. Big bluegills aren't the feisty little guys we caught when we were kids, but thick, strong fish with the power and endurance to make our aging forearms ache at the end of an evening. For us, they are an endless source of fishing delight. We have learned we are not alone.

There are more bluegill lovers than we ever imagined. Granted, some are opportunists who soothe their fishing fever only during the spawn when bluegills are relatively easy. The remainder don't put away their bream flies until winter forces them off the water. They are the nursing administrator who casts exuberantly from her pontoon boat, the repairman who tediously threads his way through nasty briars to his favorite stretch of the river, and the retired teacher who discovers wealth every now and then in a pond that bass students abandoned. Mention bluegills to bluegill lovers and they will tell you with a great big smile that it's pure fun. That's the source of our devotion—the fun.

Reading *Bluegill Fly Fishing & Flies* will help you catch more and larger bluegill. "More" and "larger" are relative terms dependent upon many factors. More is vastly different when comparing the spawning season to the expected results of fishing a hot August afternoon. A six-inch fish taken from a tiny rivulet might be equal in its uniqueness to a twelve-inch specimen that makes its home in a prime southern pond. "More" and "larger" must be defined within the context of the circumstances.

It must be noted that neither the number of fish caught nor their size should negatively impact the quality of the fishing experience. Don't become discouraged about catching eight-inch bluegill when the water is known to produce twelve-inchers. Enjoy the fight, then release the fighter.

Despite qualifying our terms, we can set some standards based upon our experiences.

How Many Is More?

During the height of the spring spawn, forty to eighty fish is about average for a good-producing area. One-hundred-fish days are not uncommon, but let's remember spawning fish are the most concentrated, most aggressive, and easiest to catch.

The dog days of summer are very different. Highly selective fish have retreated to deeper cover. Anglers who persist in pounding the shoreline shallows that produced so well for them in the spring will locate few bluegills. A knowledgeable fly-fisher who understands the needs of bluegills will usually be able to locate and catch fifteen to thirty or more during this tough time of year.

How Large Is Large?

Despite the wide variety of waters in which bluegills thrive, it is surprisingly simple to determine the average large size that any given water may produce. During the spawn, the largest fish will be the most aggressive in defending territory. If you are fishing the spawning beds carefully, the larger fish caught are the average of the largest available. That doesn't discount the presence of some rare monsters that are several year classes older. That phenomenon is always possible for any species in any body of water.

Bluegills are sized from tiny to fifteen or sixteen inches. In our home state of Missouri, four to eight years are required to grow bluegills of eight inches. A record-size specimen of fifteen inches would require both unusual longevity and remarkable food availability.

We have chosen eight inches as the standard for "larger." Ten-inchers should be reason for compliments from your fishing partner, fish twelve inches and larger are cause for celebration.

Let's Check the Records

The National Fresh Water Fishing Hall of Fame, located in Hayward, Wisconsin, serves as a clearinghouse for record catches of all freshwater species. Examining the 1997 edition of their national and state records for bluegills is revealing and provides some surprises.

The North American record bluegill is a 4-pound, 12-ounce monster caught in April of 1950 in Ketona Lake, Alabama, by T. S. Hudson. Two other states—Kentucky and North Carolina—also have produced bluegills over four pounds. Seventeen more states have produced bluegills in excess of three pounds. Surprisingly, three southern states—Florida, Oklahoma, and Arkansas—have managed state records only in the two-pound range. Of course, state conservation departments, and subsequently the Hall of Fame, can only record those fish which are verified and reported to them. It is plausible that larger fish have been caught in each of these southern states but were not submitted as record catches.

The coded map on the facing page shows a large band of states extending from South Dakota east to New Jersey and south to Alabama where the record bluegills exceed three pounds. Does this reveal the location of our nation's best large-bluegill fishing, or does it tell us that this section of the country takes its bluegill fishing more seriously?

While this information may be valuable in indicating where some of the largest bluegills are located, it doesn't tell us how they were taken. After checking the Hall of Fame North American fly-fishing records, we suspect that not many state bluegill records were set by anglers using fly rods. The fly-fishing record is a two-

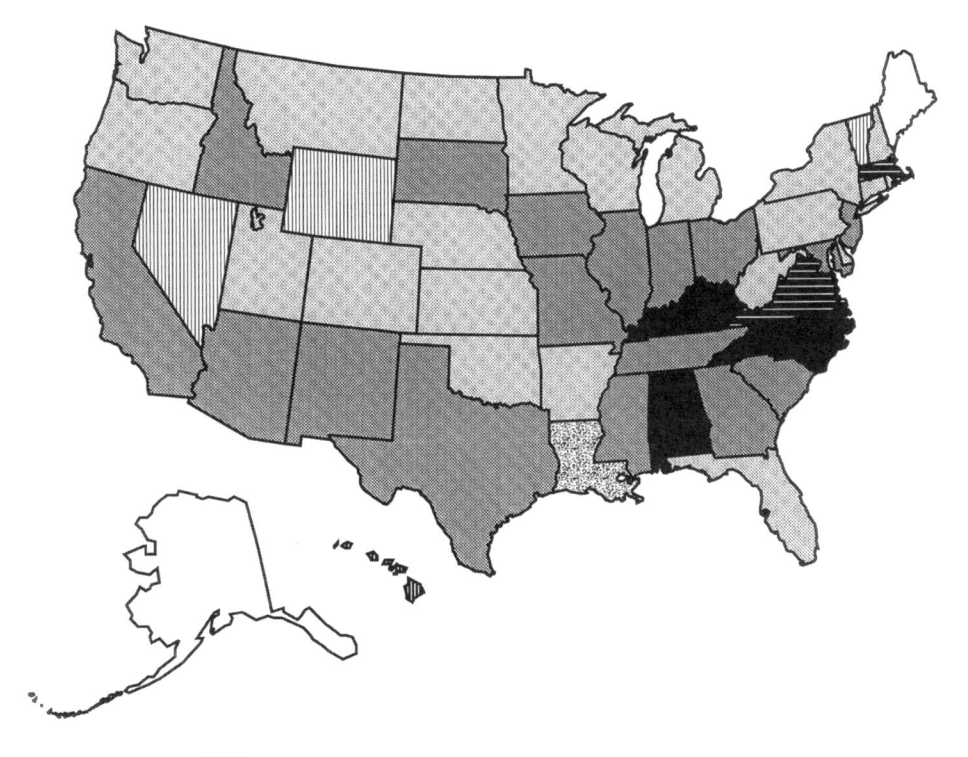

☐ NO BLUEGILL RECORDS
≡ RECORDS LISTED AS SUNFISH
    NOT AS BLUEGILL SEPARATELY
▦ UNDER ONE POUND
▥ ONE POUND
▦ TWO POUNDS
▦ THREE POUNDS
■ FOUR POUNDS
▦ OPEN CATEGORY

pound fish taken in October of 1994 from a farm pond in Arkansas by Michael Robert Stout using eight-pound tippet. It may be that fly-fishers are more inclined to release their fish and consequently are less likely to report a record catch.

Recently, the Hall of Fame has initiated a category for catch-and-release records that requires only length measurements and not official weights. This is commendable because most, if not all, of the previous record fish had to be killed to be authenticated as records.

One thing is certain—none of those dead fish grew larger, nor did other anglers enjoy the thrill of catching them.

Curiously, the Hall of Fame does not have a catch-and-release record for bluegills. We strongly urge fly-fishers to rectify that glaring omission.

"Dead fish" records should remain static symbols of our own enlightenment. In the future, we hope catch-and-release records will increase for all species, including our beloved bluegill.

Why Use a Fly Rod?

Frequently, fly rodding is the most productive method of fishing. There are several reasons for this bonus attraction to the sport. First, the fly rod is capable of laying a minute concoction of feathers on the water with the gentleness of a lover's whisper. Bait-casting, spinning and spin-casting equipment must rely on the weight of the lure to pull line from the reel. Anything with the mass to do that must be accompanied by a considerable splashdown with little subtlety. Flies enter the bluegill's world like natural prey. Casting plugs cannot.

Second, flies spend more time where the fish are. When a fly has been retrieved, it's simply and quickly picked up and recast into more productive water. A bait-casting or spinning angler must reel in the lure until it dangles within inches of the rod tip. In the course of a day's fishing, lures spend a sizable amount of time in fishless water. Based on that fact alone, more fish are likely to see and, therefore, hit a fly which remains in their bailiwick.

Finally, the hook-set is cushioned by the springiness of the long, limber fly rod. This is a considerable advantage when the quarry has a soft, fleshy mouth that can be easily torn by even a moderate hook-set from the bait-caster.

We have fished with nearly all of the known sportfish-catching devices and confess we didn't dislike any of them. For us, the fly rod provides the most pleasure. Too often with other methods, satisfaction suffers when fish-catching slows.

The fly rod won't allow that. The cast must be rhythmic, gentle, and smooth. Even when fish-catching slows, our enjoyment doesn't. The need within us for artful expression, as well as our pragmatic interest in pure fish catching, is fulfilled best by the fly rod.

The World's Most Enjoyable Sportfish

For nearly every conceivable reason, bluegills are the fly rodder's perfect fish.

Also known as bream (pronounced brim) in the southern United States, our subject is the true bluegill. We're not concerned with green, redear or longear sunfish, nor any of the other thirty members of the family Centrarchidae, although their ranges frequently overlap and anglers often confuse their proper identifications.

The bluegill's Latin moniker is *Lepomis macrochirus*, but that's all the taxonomy you'll get from us. Our objective is not to classify but to catch bluegills. To that end, we are disdainful of the term "sunfish." It's a misnomer. Small young-of-the-year bluegills school heavily in the sunlit shallows, but it's the largest of the species that hold our interest. As with the giants of any warmwater species, these brutes tend to occupy the best lies, utilize the heaviest cover, and seek the deepest shadows.

We expect game fish to provide the thrills of a good fight, enough difficulty in their capture to let us believe we've outwitted them, and physical characteristics that make them unique.

Judging the fighting merits of any game fish requires definition of the tackle used in its conquest. The fight of a ten-pound largemouth bass wouldn't feel special when caught on a deep-sea rod and reel used to subdue marlin and giant tuna. Similarly, the fight of a one-pound bluegill is lost on bait-casting gear and twenty-pound-test line.

The bluegill's short, compact body, and its penchant for pulling at right angles to the angler's pressure make it a tenacious fighter. Those who mock the bluegill's fighting ability have caught them on equipment that was too heavy, or have caught only smaller fish. Often, a nice-sized bluegill's fight is waged in minute circles which prevent the angler from bringing it directly to hand, and this fighting technique has endeared *Lepomis macrochirus* to generations of admirers. Yet, most of the large ones we've encountered—those in the nine-inch-and-beyond category—have fought quite differently. These largest of their kind tend to make strong runs into deep water when hooked. We've often heard it said that a five-pound bream could not be handled on conventional tackle. We heartily agree, but would love to give it our best effort just the same.

In angling literature, writers exalt the beauty of their favored species. We recognize that each has a beauty all its own, like the bronze-colored smallmouth or the blue-haloed red spots and vermiculated back of a brook trout. Bluegills need not be humbled by the coloration of any other species. Depending on the water from which it's taken, its body color may vary from subtle, shaded yellow through a range of olives to deep, dark blue. Those taken from nutrient-deficient water, as is found in some quarry ponds, are almost transparent. Usually, the sides of the bluegill's body are marked by several irregular vertical bars. The gill flap is black, with turquoise along the lower jaw. The breast ranges from pale yellow to bright orange on male fish. These intense colors are usually thought to be reserved for tropical fish, but the bluegill angler touches a piece of rainbow with each catch.

To most of the fishing community, the bluegill's most surprising characteristic is its selectivity. Most folks who chase other species to the exclusion of bluegills condemn bream as too easy to capture. Younger fish, which spend all day schooled in the shallows, will feed on anything that fits into their mouths and attack much of what will not. Spawning bluegills, involved in protecting their colonies and fry, throw caution to the wind and also are easily caught. Larger summertime fish, however, can be extremely difficult. It is our opinion that large summer bluegills are freshwater's most selective fish.

Our observations clearly indicate that bluegills customarily approach their prospective meals from behind, then either hesitate or trail their prey as if evaluating the meal. If all seems well, they rush forward to grab the morsel.

We have often observed the bream's lightning-quick expulsion of any suspicious item. Watching this reaction leads us to suspect that we often receive hits that are completely undetected. This lesson would seem to indicate an increased need to watch more vigilantly for even the most subtle line hesitations.

The most convincing evidence of bluegill selectivity comes from fishing experiences. Frequently, when one of us begins to catch large bluegills, the other will fish the same leader length and count the fly to the same depth but use another color, pattern, size, or other fly variation such as action, shape, and sound. It is remarkable how often in the summer season the fish will focus on a very narrow band of acceptable offerings. Sometimes the flies we use are not very representative, at least in our eyes, of any natural prey in their environment. It is further significant that, of the factors we've tested, size and action are most consistently important to success.

Whether due to genetic makeup or learned response, it seems clear to us that larger summer bluegills epitomize the term, "selective."

The bluegill's propensity for feeding on or near the surface is one of its most endearing qualities, not only ensuring the conventional fly-caster easy accessibility, but also enhancing the enjoyment of catching fish. And, it once again tilts the odds in favor of the fly-fisher.

Some would dismiss the bream as a non-jumper while lauding the acrobatics of smallmouth or largemouth bass and trout. Although it is true that bluegills don't often leap during the fight, it does occur. We have experienced it on a number of occasions, and have concluded that it is accidental. In those instances, it appeared the fish were simply "aimed" at the surface when they made a last, desperate thrust for freedom. It did not seem to be an effort to throw the hook as occurs with other species.

Perhaps the reason for the bluegill's relatively infrequent jumps is a result of body shape more than a predisposition to fight a deeper battle. Its short, rather flat body favors the use of angles and water pressure against the surface of its body to provide resistance. For us, this offers a superior fight because most of the action occurs within the upper two or three feet of water and is usually quite visible.

As with other surface-feeding fish, bluegills feed more than ninety percent of the time beneath the water's surface. Still, we, like most anglers, spend a disproportionate amount of time pursuing them on top. There appears to be a dry-fly soul in each of us.

Sheer abundance may provide the best motivation for pursuing bluegills. Despite the popular concept that the fly-fisher's world should consist of pastoral streams and sleek trout, there just isn't a good supply of either. Those of us fortunate enough to live in trout country recognize that, all too often, the pools we had planned to fish are occupied and the fish, especially the wild ones, are scarce. Each year, more free-flowing streams succumb to bulldozers and concrete while our burgeoning population seeks the solitude that streams provide. Creating new streams is prohibitively expensive and best left in the hands of a higher power.

But there is a solution. Impounded waters and bluegills can provide an almost limitless supply of grand fly fishing. Ponds are relatively easily and inexpensively created, and the prolific reproductive capabilities of the bluegill can provide wonderful sport for us. A single female bluegill can lay up to 38,000 eggs, and the species has been observed to spawn up to nine times in a single season. While it is essential that we continue to conserve and protect all the species and waters we have left, it is clear that the bluegill is the species for our increasingly overcrowded future.

As an abundant game fish, bream are valuable because nearly everyone in the United States has nearby access to them. For a considerable period of our lives, we lived six hours from the nearest trout stream. This meant our trout-fishing forays were confined to occasional weekend and vacation trips to faraway destinations. Often our journeys became exercises in frustration. When too many people had the same experience in mind, or when the fish became fickle, locals would chide us with, "You should have been here last week."

Bluegills, though, were never more than half a mile away. They were available to us any evening after work or any day we could find free time. Because they are so adaptable, bluegills are probably nearer to most anglers than they realize. Natural lakes, sprawling impoundments, farm ponds or stock tanks, sloughs, bayous, flowages, strip-mine pits, and city water-supply lakes all provide bluegill fishing. In addition, there are drainage ditches, ox-bow lakes, city-park ponds, rivers, streams, creeks, even storm sewers that hold surprising populations of *Lepomis macrochirus*. They can be pursued on a daily basis and provide angling thrills for young and old, expert and novice, wader and powerboater, float-tuber and wheelchair-bound angler. They are near urban, suburban, and country dwellers alike.

If you want to fish more frequently and use light rods with fine tippets to catch more fish, the bluegill is the species for you.

Beautiful Vibrations: The Story of Buddy

Over three decades ago, the eldest of us began a public-school teaching career in a tiny northeast Missouri hamlet. Within minutes of arriving for duty, a freckle-faced youngster whose job description apparently included the elimination of neophyte instructors was encountered. His name was Buddy.

Autumn, winter, and early spring were spent in combat with Buddy, and classroom control was maintained only by the narrowest of margins. Finally, with the outcome still very much in doubt, Buddy's presence was requested after class.

"Yeah, whadidodistime?" he sneered.

An invitation to go fishing was extended. Narrow slits which had passed for eyes opened only slightly, and a smile invaded one corner of his mouth. Fifteen-year-old seventh graders can be very cynical.

"You serious?" he asked, lifting an eyebrow.

After receiving appropriate assurances, Buddy's eyes sparkled, and the grin he wore infected his whole body. Thrusting one fist in the air, he ran through the crowded hallway shouting, "Awright!"

With the trip scheduled for the following day after classes, his absence from school was surprising, yet dismissed as another lost opportunity to communicate with the belligerent youngster. As the day's final bell echoed through the hall, Buddy appeared in the parking lot. One jaw was grotesquely swollen from a double dose of chewing tobacco, the pockets of his bib overalls were stuffed with snacks and even more tobacco products, and he held a dilapidated cigar box containing every conceivable fishing contrivance then known in one hand and a rusted five-and-a-half-foot steel casting rod in the other. It was obvious he had spent the entire day preparing for the outing.

Buddy's equipment served him badly and, recognizing his attention was slipping, a spare fly rod was quickly pieced together. In ten minutes he was casting without major difficulty despite a guidance counselor's warning that he possessed significant learning deficiencies. Soon we were both catching hand-sized bluegills repeatedly.

On the ride home, Buddy shared his thoughts about his first experience with a fly rod. "Man," he enthused, "I jus' luv them bee-you-tee-ful vi-ber-ray-shuns." With the eloquence of a poet, Buddy had captured the essence of the fly-fisher's world. It is, in fact, those "beautiful vibrations" that cause us to pursue game fish with a long and limber rod.

Thank you, Buddy, wherever you are.

Chapter 2
GEARING UP

> "I BELIEVE THE REWARDS THAT WE DERIVE FROM OUR FISHING ARE DIRECTLY PROPORTIONAL TO THE LEVEL OF SOPHISTICATION THAT WE APPLY TO IT."
>
> Jack Ellis
> *The Sunfishes*
> ©1993, Abenaki Publishers, Inc.
> Bennington, Vermont

Gearing Up

One of the most enchanting aspects of fly fishing for bluegills is that it can be as simple or as complex as you want it to be. A rod, reel, line, leader, and a handful of flies can put anyone in the action. Absolutely nothing else is necessary. Entry-level expenses are minimal, and are certainly less than most other recreational pursuits.

Emphasis should be placed on a balanced outfit. A rod is designed to cast line of a specific weight or density ranging in size from number zero (extremely light) to number fifteen (extremely heavy). This number is often, but not always, found on the butt section of the fly rod. The line weight must match the weight of the rod or be one weight greater than the specified rod weight. Most who have tried and given up fly casting have done so because of unbalanced equipment.

Fly line can actually be cast without the benefit of a rod but it is not a pleasant experience. Only when the weight of the line is correctly matched to cause the proper flexing action of the rod does the casting process become nearly effortless and satisfying.

To many, an uncomplicated approach is very appealing. For the rest of us who are fascinated by gadgets and conveniences, there are catalogs and fly shops full of accessory items. For those new to the sport of fly fishing or those new to the sport of bluegill fly fishing, here is more information about equipment.

Rods

Fly rods made from fiberglass and bamboo can perform acceptably. Fiberglass rods are durable and inexpensive, but quite heavy. Bamboo rods are also heavy and may be prohibitively expensive. Modern rods constructed of lightweight graphite are far superior casting and fishing tools, and are available in a wide price range. The beginning bluegill fly-fisher is best advised to purchase an eight- to nine-foot rod designed to carry six- or seven-weight line. This is an excellent all-around fishing tool because it enables the caster to handle the full range of fly sizes from tiny, weightless dries to rather bulky, weighted offerings with wind-resistant wings and tails. For the bluegill fisher's needs, eight-weight and heavier rods are unnecessary.

Two considerations prevail in rod-weight choice. One is the size and wind-resistance of the fly being cast, the other is the cover being fished. We would land few large fish casting over thick entanglements of brush and tree limbs or aquatic vegetation with a two-weight rod, yet, no one could deny the pleasures of using light equipment in areas that are clear of sub-aquatic debris. We frequently fish with three-weight outfits.

Rod length may also be adjusted to the conditions being fished. Longer rods are advantageous where higher backcasts are important. For fishing where there are tall plants on the bank in the backcast, float-tubing, seated boat fishermen and for roll-casting, use of eight- to nine-foot rods is encouraged.

Short rods have an advantage when overhanging tree branches canopy the stream or pond, and when brushy conditions only allow anglers to poke the rod through the branches and dip the fly on or in the water.

The rod's "action" is another important consideration. This is determined mainly by the flexibility of the rod's tip section. Some rods are designed to flex less than others. We refer to these rods as having "fast" action because the timing of the casting stroke is quicker. Other rods are manufactured with a softer, more flexible action which requires a slower casting stroke. Rod action is, in our view, a personal choice dependent upon individual style. Those buying a rod for the first time should try many different rod actions, preferably under the watchful eye of an experienced caster. While the buyer will soon discover which feels most comfortable, an experienced observer can watch for tailing loops, which occur when the rod tip is stopped above the path of the fly line. This may indicate the need for a faster rod. In addition, the experienced observer should ask questions regarding the situations the buyer intends to fish, thereby personalizing the rod to a greater extent.

The rod is the most important piece of equipment a fly-fisher possesses. It will give countless hours of pleasure both in casting and in enhancing the beautiful vibrations of catching fish. In addition, with reasonable care it may last a lifetime and become a beautiful gift to a grandchild when the angler has made his last cast. Buy the best you can reasonably afford.

Reels

A single-action reel large enough to hold the fly line is suitable for bluegill fly fishing, as we've not yet encountered the bluegill capable of pulling out all the line. Still, there is value in loading the spool to capacity because it enlarges the spool diameter, resulting in a faster retrieve and preventing the line from being stored in small, kinky loops.

Usually one hundred yards of twenty-pound-test, braided-Dacron backing on the rear of the line will perform this function, in addition to inexpensively allowing the one-outfit owner the flexibility of pursuing other species. A spare spool is necessary if sink-tip or full-sinking lines are to be used. We use floating lines much of the time, but the summer season on big reservoirs is a major exception. Here, we often fish full-sinking lines to get down to the bigger bluegills that frequently locate against steep bluffs or in submerged wood in depths of eight feet or more.

The budget-conscious fly-fisher can economize on the reel. Since its primary function is line storage, as opposed to fly delivery, they need not be expensive. Durability and smoothness, however, should not be compromised, nor should the weight of the reel be excessive. So-called automatic reels are far too heavy to warrant serious consideration, and those with which we've experimented either malfunctioned or were in the process of doing so.

Fly Lines

Too often, beginning fly-fishers purchase expensive rods and reels only to choose a cheap, level fly line from a discount store. Unfortunately, they cannot discover the pure joy of effortless fly-casting and are probably destined to quit the sport in disgust. Start with a weight-forward floating fly line of good quality. Some prefer light-colored or even fluorescent lines simply because they are easier to see. This choice enables the fisherman to detect strikes more easily and to see the line in the casting process. Both are helpful in learning fly-line control.

Modern fly lines need very little attention. They will accumulate dried moss and dirt, but non-abrasive soap and warm water or fly-line cleanser applied occasionally will keep them performing well. Avoid contact with things that can cut or abrade the line and do not allow them to be stored in full sunlight. Excessive heat and ultraviolet light will damage the line. With minimal care good fly line will last through several seasons of fishing for most people.

For an extra spool of fly line, a good quality medium-sinking shooting taper may be the best choice. That is the recommendation of Mel Krieger, (*The Essence of Flycasting*, ©1987, Club Pacific, San Francisco) one of the world's foremost teachers of fly casting who advises, "Casting with this denser, smaller-diameter line will familiarize you with the faster timing needed for sinking fly lines."

Krieger further advises that this shooting taper be one size larger than your floating line. "The increased weight makes it easier to get the maximum load (bend) in the rod . . . " Use sinking line only with rods designed for six-weight lines and heavier. To do so with lighter rods defeats their purpose.

The end of the fly line should either have a braided loop end cemented securely in place or be nail-knotted to a heavy monofilament butt section, the end of which can be tied in a perfection loop or a Duncan loop knot. The Duncan loop knot, however, may slip under pressure. The end loop in either case enables the easy attachment of a leader and also allows it to be quickly changed.

Leaders

Leaders are the nearly invisible connecting material that transmits the energy of the cast to the fly. They vary widely in length, but a monofilament leader of seven and one-half to nine feet will handle most situations. Knotless tapered leaders perform best for bluegill fishing. They will not pick up moss and weed pieces as knotted leaders are prone to do.

An alternative to monofilament leaders are those made of braided nylon. They are very supple, and turn over easily even with short, soft casts. Some reject their use because they wind-knot easily, which adversely affects their usefulness. Their strength, while sometimes an asset, inhibits breaking off the tippet when the leader itself has snagged sturdy branches and submerged weed stems.

Long leaders are necessary when casting to spooky fish in clear water. Sometimes leaders of twelve to fifteen feet are used to present delicate dry flies under demanding circumstances. Likewise, exceptionally short leaders also have a use. When using sink-tip and full-sinking lines, the leader must be shortened to prevent it from bowing back toward the surface, which neutralizes the advantage of sinking line. In these circumstances, we often use leaders of three feet or less by cutting back from the butt end of the leader to the desired length and tying a perfection loop or a Duncan loop knot in the new leader's butt end.

Many otherwise proficient fly-fishers handicap themselves by trying to nurse a leader through an entire season by constantly adding tippet material. Unless you are an expert in correctly proportioning leader section lengths, this is probably a mistake. Why take chances with the final link in your fly-delivery system? When leader price is compared to the cost of everything else, it just doesn't make sense to become miserly about changing leaders.

Tippet Materials

It is important to carry a range of tippet material sizes so that adaptations can be made to each fishing situation. With today's new super-strong nylon and fluorocarbon tippet material, it is possible to have high tensile strength (pound-test) and relatively thin diameter line.

While this is generally good, it is important to have enough diameter to enable bulky and weighted flies to turn over effectively. We carry tippet spools from 0X to 7X. Because large bluegills can be very leader shy, the thinner diameter tippets are especially necessary when fishing dry flies in clear waters. It is important, however, to use the strongest tippet the conditions will allow because most big bluegills are found in or near tough cover.

There is a variety of tippet spool-carrying devices and dispensers. We prefer the stackable spools which snap together and are easily replaced when emptied.

Leader-sink

Even when fishing dry flies, it's preferable that the leader sink so as not to allow a fish-alarming shadow. With sinking flies, a floating leader inhibits the countdown of weighted offerings. Products that promote leader sinking are helpful, and reduce leader flash as well. Pond mud will work, too, but there will be gritty abrasives in it which damage the leader, and it will wash off quickly.

Leader Straightener

Leaders are packaged and stored on our reels in small loops. Trying to cast these coiled leaders can be frustrating because the fly seems to acquire a mind of its own. The leader will remain in that condition until we take steps to straighten it. The solution is really quite simple. When monofilament is pulled between two pieces of rubber it straightens beautifully. A small, folded-over piece of old bicycle inner tube will do the job, but leather-clad commercial models are inexpensive and, when attached to fishing vests on a small retractable pin-on reel, are easily accessible.

Floatant

For flies designed to ride atop the water's surface, floatant is an important aid. Pastes, granules, liquids, and spray-ons all do an effective job of keeping flies afloat. We prefer sprays for standard dry flies because they are quick, easy, and not messy to use. The pastes mat the hackles together, but do tend to remain effective longer. We use pastes when little deer hair poppers and divers become waterlogged and need a refresher.

Vests

Fly-fishers inevitably acquire a considerable arsenal of flies and a wide assortment of accessory items, each of which acquires indispensable status. This necessitates an equipment carrier. Fly-fishing legend Lee Wulff recognized this problem decades ago and designed a vest with many pockets to solve the problem. Comfortable and lightweight, Lee's vest safely transported all the fishing tackle he needed.

Fishing vests have since become more complex and heavier, yet they remain a practical solution for the walking, wading, and float-tubing angler. Some are designed for use in summer's heat and are constructed of nylon mesh which allows for air penetration, others utilize materials for warmth and some are water repellent. There are even models which incorporate an inflatable chamber to be used as a floatation safety device for the wading angler. Vests come in a wide range of colors and designs, and the suitability of each depends upon the user. A fly-fisher's vest soon becomes his most personalized piece of equipment. Only the owner knows which little pocket contains the needed item.

Fly fishing's lightweight gear is ideal for the bank-bound angler.

Boat Bags

For the fly-fisher who spends considerable time in boats, the vest is a less desirable solution. Because the vest is more restrictive and cumbersome to the seated angler, it is eventually discarded. This makes finding the needed accessory more difficult, and subjects the vest-held items to the abuse of the boat bottom, including the puddle of water which inevitably seems to accumulate there. Boating anglers are much better served by a boat bag.

A functional boat bag should be durable (canvas or Cordura fills the bill) and have a carrying handle, shoulder strap, or both. It should be lightweight and padded to protect the valuables inside, and should be compartmentalized and have zipped or Velcro-closured pockets on the outside.

We're acquainted with one fly-fisher who fishes exclusively from a boat and uses a large plastic tackle box designed for bait-casting plugs. The box has a series of drawers which he labels and it seems to work well for him, but the thought of overturning that tackle box is nightmarish. Whatever system or combination of gear-toting you choose, there will be an ever-increasing volume of contents. Be sure your system is expandable.

Fly Boxes

Fly boxes are constructed of a wide variety of materials, from hand-crafted exotic woods to plastic and metal. Some are simple, open spaces while others have magnetic posts, rippled foam, or springs to hold hooks securely in place. The most elaborate are constructed with small transparent lids to be individually lifted using a tiny lever. The transparent top enables the angler to view the flies in compartments while selecting the correct pattern.

Some prefer fly boxes that are breathtakingly expensive while others use boxes and tubes designed for other purposes altogether. Several years ago, a national fly-fishing magazine published an interesting article about the contents of Lee Wulff's vest. His fly boxes weren't, as one might imagine, the finest hand-crafted wood boxes with intricate glass lids. Instead, the most respected of fly-fishers had chosen empty cough-drop tins to carry his flies. Each hinged metal box contained a different fly type (dries, nymphs, emergers).

As with any object, of course, pride of ownership cannot be discounted. The fancy boxes are both beautiful and functional, but our system differs only slightly from Mr. Wulff's. We purchase the compartmentalized, see-through plastic boxes found in most discount and crafts stores, and identify the contents of each box using an inexpensive hand-operated labeler.

Sunglasses

Protective eye wear should be required equipment for all fly-casters. The tiny, weighted hooks attached to the end of our leaders are sometimes errantly cast even by the most proficient casters. It is not worth the risk of damaging or losing your vision. Even on overcast days when sunglasses are not necessary, it is a good practice to carry and use a pair of clear plastic safety glasses.

Beyond the role of protection, however, good polarized sunglasses can provide a window beneath the surface for the fisherman. This can be invaluable in locating fish and understanding fish behavior.

Magnifying Lenses

For those of us who have reached the age when the threading and tying process has become a group project, magnifying lenses truly are a gift from heaven. Clear plastic magnifying lenses make this task as simple as it used to be, and the lenses attach either to regular glasses or a hat brim. They conveniently flip out of the way when not needed. If you're spending too much time fooling with terminal tackle, magnifying lenses will be as important to you as your flies.

Flex Light

Low-light periods are times of heightened insect activity when bluegills are more active, too. Yet, fly selection and knot tying are much more difficult. A flex light is a tiny battery-operated flashlight with a movable head that can be aimed at the work area you select.

Hook Hone

Even new hooks aren't always as sharp as we'd like, and when they're pulled across rocks and snags, dullness is easy to understand. A small hook hone kept in a vest pocket solves the problem.

Hook Disgorger/Pliers

All bluegill mouths are too small to accommodate hook removal with human fingers, and it is sometimes necessary to gently remove a deeply taken fly. Rather than risk injury to the fish, a good pair of surgical forceps not only handles this problem adequately, but can also serve as a debarbing tool when that task has been omitted at the tying vise. Barbless hooks not only enable us to release more fish unharmed, but also provide an easier penetration on the hook-set.

Tape Measure

Bluegill size should be expressed in length, not weight. Perhaps all fish should be judged in this manner. Weighing a fish precisely requires quite a lot of handling and since most in-the-field weighing devices are so notoriously inaccurate, the clear implication is that the fish must die in order for us to weigh it properly.

This is most unacceptable. If we carry a small tape measure it becomes a simple matter to quickly get an accurate length reading. Having done so, when we say that we caught an eleven-inch bluegill, everyone knows how large the fish actually was. That great fish can quickly and safely be returned to the water to thrill other anglers.

Waders

There are lots of style and material options when choosing waders. We prefer chest waders of a lightweight but durable material in the stocking-foot style. The lightweight waders enable wading when it is too cool to wet wade and, by layering clothing, it is still possible to wade when it is downright chilly. Separate boots allow us to use the boots alone while wet-wading or wet-tubing. We find lightweight waders the only reasonable alternative in the summer when we are wading mucky ponds that may have submerged trees or old fences.

Because our waders are always subjected to lots of abuse, we choose less expensive ones, knowing that in two to four seasons they'll have to be replaced. Wading shoes should be chosen carefully for fit, comfort, and durability. We prefer felt-soled boots because we often fish streams with rocky bottoms. They are a bit of a problem, however, in slick, mud-bottomed ponds and on wet, grassy slopes. The felt soles act like a pair of skis on mud and wet grass, and the wearer can slip and slide around dangerously. Moving slowly and sliding your feet helps only a little. If your fishing pretty much excludes rocky areas, you would be better served by rubber-soled boots.

Wader Belt, Wading Staffs, and Inflatable Suspenders and Vests

Over the years, we've taken some death-defying spills. Most were due to our own lack of caution. It is easy to advise respect for the water, but good advice is just as easily forgotten when rising fish are the focus of attention. A wader belt tightened around the waist to prevent water from filling the waders is a necessity.

A wading staff, whether a hand-cut sapling or fancy commercial version, can be a tremendous aid. Most of our accidental dunkings have seemed to unfold in slow motion. If we had supported ourselves with the use of a staff, almost all could have been eliminated.

Inflatable suspenders and vests are another option. They are lightweight and easily worn, and inflate to provide instant floatation when the rip-cord is pulled. They function by utilizing replaceable CO_2 cartridges, and are useful to wading and float-tubing anglers alike.

Float Tubes

There are many float tubes from which to choose. Even as youngsters, we recognized the advantage of reaching waters other anglers could not fish. Using an old car tire inner tube with a board across the middle as a seat and a paddle for propulsion gave us that access but, clearly, the apparatus lacked style. In the early seventies, we purchased a molded-plastic model. It was a bit heavy and cumbersome to carry but it was a marvelous improvement. Eventually it split in the seat seam. We tried everything from fiberglass repair kits to aerosol cans of foam to correct the problem, but nothing worked very long. The donut would take on water until it became dangerously tipsy. Sadly, we had to discard it.

Today's inflatable, non-rotting nylon models incorporate comfortable seats, lots of storage space, backrests, even casting aprons to serve as work areas to keep loose fly line from dangling into the water, entangling feet and fins. Most have rulers for measuring fish incorporated into the design. In effect, float tubes enable the fly-caster to fish from a very comfortable chair.

Price tends to reflect quality in choosing the right tube. All the additional amenities, like carrying handles, extra storage space, and Velcro tabs to secure the rod while the fisherman changes flies, increase the already considerable pleasure of float-tubing.

Fellow big-bluegill aficionado, Deke Meyer, author of *Float Tube Fly Fishing* (c1989, Frank Amato Publications), explains the effectiveness of float tubing this way:

"Quietly finning along will get you closer to more stillwater fish and bigger ones, too, because you are a silent stalker. There are not built-in noisemakers in a float tube—no resonating aluminum hull, no clanking of metal or rubbing of wood."

We also use our float tubes in slow-moving streams to access areas unreachable by wading anglers. Whether in still or moving water, it is good practice to float tube with a partner and to use either a life jacket or inflatable suspenders for safety.

Canoes

Canoes are comparatively lightweight and can be car-topped or portaged into off-road waters inaccessible to many. They are especially adaptable as a maneuverable and portable vehicle for floating streams because they can be dropped at one river access and easily taken out at one further downstream. On the other hand, canoes are not built for stability and, if you have difficulty casting from a seated position without rocking back and forth, they would not be a good fishing craft for you.

It is best to beach the canoe and wade slackwater areas preferred by bluegills before moving downstream to the next productive area. Be careful to secure any items that could be lost if the canoe overturned. Rods can be fastened to the seats and thwarts of the canoe with Velcro strips. Rod socks and cases help protect the rods in this situation.

Bluegill Boats

Fishermen have a wider selection of boats available to them now than ever before. Some are large, heavy, and well equipped. Others are small, light, and simple.

The most coveted boat style is called a bass boat. With its exceptionally stable casting platform, it could have been designed by a fly-fisher because every high-tech gadget that has been incorporated into the design of these big lake monsters is as useful to the fly rod-wielding bluegill chaser as the ardent basser.

Ordinary aluminum boats may be inexpensively customized by adding plywood platforms, carpeting, and padded swivel seats. Just as in selecting any piece of equipment, one needs to realistically assess the uses for the boat. If you intend to trailer the boat into a variety of small lakes and ponds with unimproved boat ramps, a twenty-foot fiberglass "bluegill boat" with a two-hundred horse-power motor would be a poor choice. Similarly, if you are fishing an area of large reservoirs regularly, a ten-foot aluminum car-topper powered by a three-horsepower motor is not only inadequate, but unsafe as well.

Whether walking the banks of a small farm pond armed with rod, reel, and a box of flies, or prospecting a major reservoir with a high-powered bluegill boat, electronic locator, temperature gauge, bag full of rods and reels, and stacks of fly boxes and accessories, you are embarking on a grand adventure of discovery destined to enchant and captivate you. Now that we are geared up, let's select the flies we need to fish the varied situations we are going to encounter.

Bluegill fly fishing can be as simple or as complex as you want it to be.

Chapter 3
BULLY'S BLUEGILL SPIDER

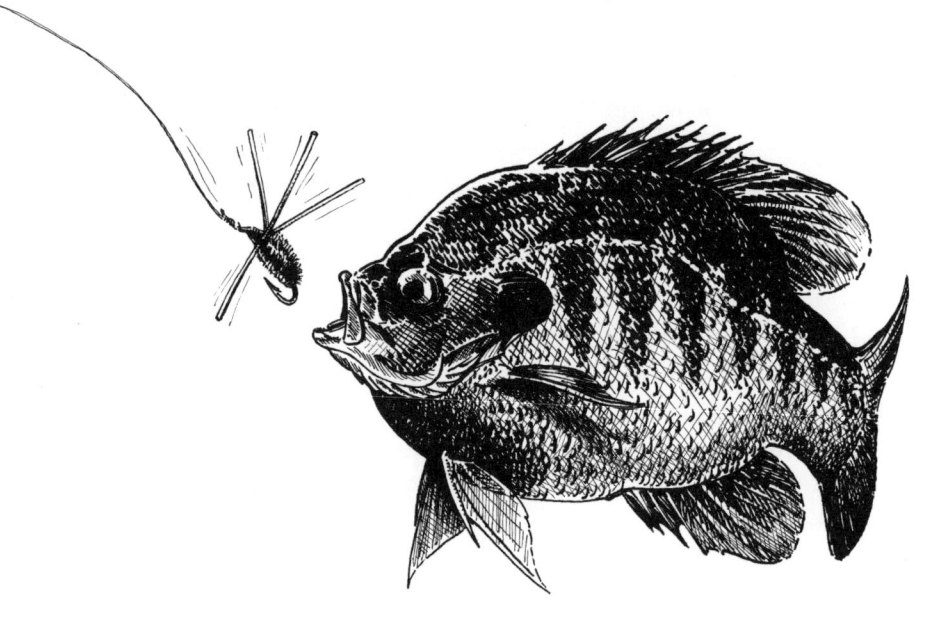

> "DON'T INSULT A FISH BY OFFERING HIM ANYTHING BUT YOUR BEST."
>
> Tom Nixon
> *Fly Tying and Fly Fishing For Bass and Panfish*
> ©1968, A. S. Barnes and Co., Inc.
> Cranbury, New Jersey

Bully's Bluegill Spider
The "Bully" Tale

On a hot, hazy summer evening in 1968, Terry closed the farm gate and walked along a familiar, dusty cow path to one of those famed "area farm ponds" locally known as a tiny bass factory. As he crested the earthen dam with his fly rod and box of deer-hair bugs, he saw an elderly cane-pole fisherman seated in the shade of a large oak tree at one corner of the pond. The smooth, dark surface was disturbed only by shallow-feeding largemouth near irregular moss beds close to shore. He strung his rod and tied a 1/0 yellow-and-black Henshall bug to his leader. He selected a pocket in the heavy moss and began false-casting to it.

Suddenly, line buzzed through the guides. He scrambled out of the mucky pond and over the earthen dam in pursuit of a young Angus bull who wore the yellow-and-black bug in the general area of its T-bone steaks. Terry's short legs were no match for the bull's four, and the chase ended abruptly with a crisp pop as the tippet snapped. He made an unceremonious landing in the dusty pasture inches from a semi-fresh cow chip.

Attempts to retrieve the deer-hair concoction were fruitless and he returned to the pond in defeat. He put away his rod and took refuge in the shade with the bluegill fisherman.

"Sorta got bullied outta yer fly, didn't ya?" smirked the cane-poler.

"Bullied is just the right word for it," Terry conceded.

The old man continued to heft chunky bluegills from a pocket in the weeds. After depositing each fish in his basket, he carefully baited his hook with another cricket.

The cricket's legs were in constant motion, discernible even when the body shape and color became indistinct. Each time, a hand-sized bluegill would appear, hesitate to evaluate his prospective meal, then suck in the juicy morsel. It was an impressive demonstration of attracting and catching large bluegills.

Our first attempts to duplicate crickets at the tying bench were miserable failures. Initially, we tied a realistic cricket, using lead wire to overcome the buoyancy of the deer hair, but field tests were not particularly successful. Some fish were caught, but not with consistency. We returned to the tying bench and produced more complex ties each time, but the bluegills still weren't impressed.

We finally learned to take our cues from the fish and made a fresh start. We decided to incorporate as much leg movement in the fly as possible, and achieve the right rate of descent through appropriately weighting the hook.

The weighting process began in the backyard swimming pool. We applied varying amounts of lead wire to our hooks, and experimented with a variety of ways of attaching it. Then we each took turns sitting on the pool bottom as the other dropped the weighted hooks into the water.

Eventually we combined the most durable method of attaching the wire with the right amount of lead, to make the fly sink at about four inches per second. Later modifications allowed the hook to sink at about a forty-five-degree angle to the water surface, hook-end first. This would become important in selecting the best position to attach the legs.

By this time, we knew the body had to be simple and streamlined to aid the fly's descent. Chenille was chosen because it would easily cover the lead wraps along the hook shank, and would absorb just enough water to enhance the fly's sinking ability. This sinkability would be offset by the attachment of wiggling legs, so the end product would sink at the same rate as our experimental model. The original model was tied with a black body, its only similarity to a real cricket.

The original legs were cut from the skirt of an old Hula Popper and splayed around the hook shank to wiggle when the fly was dropped into water. It was not a very attractive tie and the cost of Hula Popper leg material was prohibitively expensive, but the bluegills loved it. That was the only test that really mattered.

We experimented a great deal with the legs. We tried positioning them in the back, middle, and front. We attached as many as ten and as few as two. We pinned them back against the body and projected them forward for maximum mobility. We also tried legs of various lengths, and again went into the swimming pool to observe their action.

Eventually, with almost permanently wrinkled skin, we settled on four legs extended at a ninety-degree angle from the hook shank and positioned them from a point even with the hook shank. This allowed maximum gyration of rubber-hackle legs on the drop and retrieve.

Finally, the design made sense. To commemorate the strange event in the cow pasture that forever changed our bluegill fishing, we called the fly Bully's Bluegill Spider.

The end product bears no resemblance to the cricket that inspired it, but it is very durable, has a clean, simple design that presents a sharp, contrasting silhouette and, most important, has the built-in action that bluegills desire. Over the years, we have tied the fly in many colors. Bully's Bluegill Spider is effective in white, yellow, chartreuse, olive, brown, the original black, and, more recently, hot pink.

The original had white legs but we began matching the leg colors to the bodies in the early seventies. Eventually, we opted for medium, round, rubber hackle because it has just the right combination of stiffness and flexibility. No head cement is added because we believe bluegills use their sense of smell in examining their prospective meal. We do, however, double whip-finish each head to increase its durability. Because the thinner wire of a dry-fly hook is more effective in penetrating the fleshy mouths of bluegills, we use Mustad 94840 hooks. We mash down the hook's barb to reduce injury to the fish.

We have fished Bully's Bluegill Spider for many years, sharing them with friends who share our love of bluegills.

Fishing Bully Flies

The best characteristic of the Bully is that it is easy to fish. When it drops in a vertical free fall, the legs wiggle seductively. Often this is the only action necessary to attract and entice bluegills. There are, however, several retrieves we have found effective under a wide variety of conditions and fish moods. It is best to try a little of each until the bluegills indicate their preference.

By pinning the fly line to the rod with the index finger of your rod hand, it is possible to pull or strip line toward you. Two-inch strips followed by pauses of varying lengths are very effective. The quick, darting movements caused by the short strip causes the rubber legs to lurch back along the body, then, just as abruptly, return to their original angle. Each time, water movement is created which causes the flexible legs to continue to quiver slightly, even after the action has ceased. Usually the strike occurs during the pause following the strip.

Strips of six inches are effective when bluegills are especially active and in a chasing mood. The longer strip seems to simulate a food trying to escape and the competitive nature of the bluegill is stimulated by this action. Generally, the longer the strip, the longer the pause following it should last to enable the fly, which has been pulled toward the surface, to return to the fish zone.

Long strips of a foot or more, given almost continually, are surprisingly effective when slowly falling flies are ignored. While the number of occasions is comparatively few, it is still a valuable retrieve to keep in mind. We discovered it accidentally by reeling in a long cast after an evening of slow action. We can only speculate that the same escaping-prey theory applies to this situation also. Our records suggest that fish responding to this tactic usually are widely scattered and not related closely to the usual structure. It also seems these periods occur at the end of several days of stable weather.

Another effective tactic, the hand-twist retrieve, is described in detail in Chapter Seven. The hand-twist retrieve can be performed at any speed, and the action imparted to the fly ranges from a jerky, darting motion to one of constant motion.

Because Bully is weighted with five turns of .020 lead wire (that will change if lead is banned), it is important to pause a bit longer on the back cast and to throw a more open loop. It does, however, roll cast extremely well, even with soft rods. This can be important when fishing for brush-hugging bluegills.

Without reservation, Bully's Bluegill Spider is the most effective and versatile bluegill fly we have fished. While our own prejudice in that regard is understandable, it is with considerable pride that we acknowledge the plaudits of fly-fishing writers and other fishermen.

One of its endearing qualities is that it's a simple tie. If you tie your own, here is the recipe:

Bully's Bluegill Spider

Hook: Mustad 94840 or equivalent. Standard dry-fly hook, size 8-12. Mash down the barb.
Thread: Danville's 6/0 monocord or equivalent. Use color to match the body.
Underbody: .020 lead wire or equivalent.
Body: Medium chenille.
Tail: None.
Wings: Two pieces of 1 7/8-inch medium, round, rubber hackle trimmed after the fly is completed to equal lengths. After trimming, each leg is about 7/8-inch in length if tied on a size 10.
Head: Tapered, double whip-finished.

Tying "Bully" Flies

Step 1: Attach the thread just above the hook barb and wind it forward along the shank to the point at which the fly head will begin. Then, wrap back along the shank to the point where the thread was attached. This simple, but important procedure gives the hook shank a rough finish which will hold the materials securely and not allow them to slip or twist.

Step 2: Lay a piece of lead wire or other material of equal weight density along the top of, and parallel to, the hook shank and extending to within one wire width of the thread position. This will enable the final wrap of lead to miss the first line of wire, thereby creating a smoother body base.

Wrap tying thread forward to the end of the lead wire and return it to the starting point. This will enable the wire to be held in place very securely.

Next, wrap the lead wire away from you around the hook shank. Three wraps should be made within the back half of the shank. This will aid the fly in drifting downward tail-first at a forty-five-degree angle to the surface for maximum leg movement.

One transitional wrap should position the wire at the end of the lead line and the final wrap should occur off the edge of the lead line.

Now, using your dullest scissors, snip the lead wire at an angle. This creates a thin-angled lead end which can be neatly pressed around the hook shank.

Step 3: Strip 1/8 inch of the chenille end leaving exposed thread to allow for a less bulky attachment to the hook. Attach the chenille end just behind the beginning of the lead wrap at the hook bend. Wrap forward completely to the hook eye being careful to totally cover the lead. Next, place your thumbnail on top of the hook shank immediately behind the eye and apply pressure to compress the lead and chenille backward toward the hook bend just far enough to allow for wing attachment and the head. The construction of the lead wire has allowed for this process to be completed with little effort, and has created a solid base against which we will trap the rubber legs.

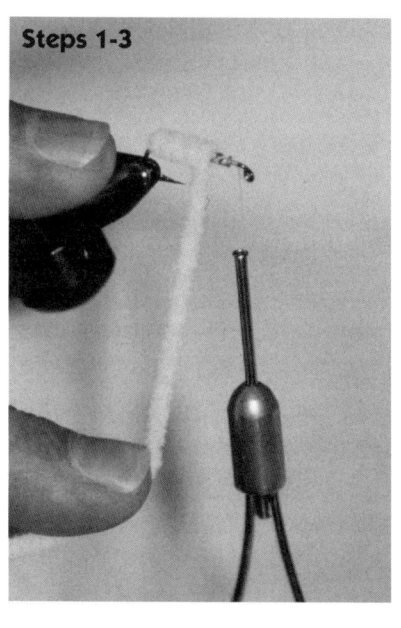

Step 4: Cut two pieces of rubber hackle to approximately 1 7/8 inches. Stack the rubber hackle so that one strand is clearly on top of the other, holding them between your thumb and index fingers while pinching them to the hook shank. Using the pinching technique, wrap the thread at the edge of the chenille, making two to three wraps to secure. Make another two to three thread wraps just in front of the rubber hackle.

Release your pinching grip on the rubber hackle and once again use your thumbnail along the top of the hook shank to compress the rubber hackle back against the chenille. If the rubber legs have been tightly trapped between the chenille and the head we are about to build, they should stand out about ninety degrees from the shank. If they are not in the right position, you can get them there by tugging gently on individual legs and also by laying a line of thread either behind or in front of the direction taken by the offending leg or legs. The legs are, at this point, infinitely adjustable by laying a line of thread behind, in front of, or between the legs for support.

Step 5: Build the head in a generally tapered manner and double whip-finish. Cut the thread at the head and trim the legs to an equal and desired length using your thumb and index fingers as general guides. Use no head cement, as bluegills evaluate their food very carefully. The finished fly resembles a spider. It looks nothing like the cricket it was originally intended to imitate, but there is no mistaking its effectiveness.

Bully's Bluegill Spider is simply the most durable and most effective bluegill fly we have ever used. It is equally productive in streams, ponds, and big reservoirs. We use it throughout the season from pre-spawn through summer and into late fall under all the weather conditions we encounter.

BLUEGILL FLY FISHING & FLIES

Chapter 4
COMPLETING THE FLY BOX

". . . THE ARTIFICIAL FLY PATTERN MAY BE THE MOST UNIQUE SPORTING ELEMENT OR TOOL MAN HAS EVER DEVELOPED."

Lefty Kreh
*The Professionals' Favorite Flies Volume I—
Dry Flies, Emergers, Nymphs & Terrestrials: Lefty's Little Library of Fly Fishing*
©1993, Odysseus Editions, Inc.
Birmingham, Alabama

Completing the Fly Box

Despite our devotion to Bully's Bluegill Spider, there are thousands of useful fly patterns for bluegills from which to choose. Some represent specific foods from the bluegill's menu, while others are impressionistic, tied to represent broad categories of edible organisms. Still others are classified as attractor patterns because, while effective, they represent no real life forms. The versatile fly-fisher will want representatives of each major category and know when and how to fish them.

Virtually any piece of material lashed, however badly, to a hook of suitable size will catch a few small fish some of the time. Our mission, however, is to capture more and, a lot of the time, larger bluegills, so we'll confine this discussion only to those flies we've found to be consistently good producers. Some are fun to fish because they entice surface strikes while others are enjoyable because they match the naturals taken by bluegills. We organize our bream flies into seven categories: topwater flies, floater/divers, wet flies, nymphs, streamers, terrestrials, and a category we simply call "others."

Topwater

Topwater flies are designed to float. Some float because they're tied of buoyant materials such as cork, closed-cell foam, and deer or elk hair. Others float because of the way they're constructed. The stiff hackle of a prime rooster neck tied to flare away from the hook shank causes the fly to ride the surface because the hackles prevent the fly from breaking through the surface tension. We employ four styles of topwater flies—cork poppers, deer-hair bugs, sponge spiders, and standard dry flies.

Cork poppers have cupped, flat, round, or tapered heads. Poppers with round or tapered heads, called sliders, are designed to create less surface disturbance.

Good-quality cork poppers should be durable and high-floating. Avoid discount-store poppers as they may lie on their sides or even sink. They may be less expensive but they aren't up to the job. Instead, stick to name brands.

The original cork popper was the creation of E. H. Peckinpaugh, a contractor from Chattanooga, Tennessee, in the early 1900s. Today, the Accardo-Peckinpaugh Company is based in Baton Rouge, Louisiana, and their poppers are still carefully tied under the watchful eye of company owner, Tony Accardo, a Southern gentleman and extraordinary bluegill fly-fisher.

We particularly like the Round Dinny, a slider, and Wildcat patterns in size 10. We use yellow and chartreuse colors most often because they are easiest to see. These patterns are especially effective when bluegills are nesting.

When fishing poppers, be careful to lift them quietly from the surface on the backcast. Ripping them off the surface causes an abnormal disturbance that will send the fish scurrying in fright for deeper water.

Deer-hair bugs perform essentially the same way as cork poppers. Some argue that their softer texture induces bluegills to hold onto them longer, thereby facilitating the hook-set. Since their main use occurs during the aggressive spawning period, however, we dismiss that claim as inconsequential, even if true. The only advantage of deer-hair bugs over poppers is the very real satisfaction that the tier receives from fishing them. Deer-hair bugs are best tied on size 8 and 10 light-wire hooks.

Sponge spiders have been around a long time, and they offer some advantages over cork and deer-hair patterns. They can be tied on smaller hooks, and they land on the water with a minimum of surface disturbance. In addition, they are exceptionally easy to tie.

Our version calls for a size 12 Mustad 94840 hook and thread to match the body color. After attaching the thread at the hook bend, we cut a V shape in the end of the closed-cell foam. Then we attach the foam at the V allowing it to lay away from the hook shank. Advancing the thread two-thirds of the hook length, we then attach two strips of small rubber hackle of about an inch in length. After tugging the legs into the desired position, we lay two or three thread wraps behind and in front to secure them. Then we bring the closed-cell foam over the top of the hook shank and secure it with two or three thread wraps just ahead of the legs. Advancing the thread, we again lash the foam to the hook with two or three wraps to form the insect's head. A few more wraps and a whip-finished head completes the tie.

This little foam spider can be tied in a variety of colors, but yellow, green, and black have worked best for us. Since it is so light and quiet in the water, we have found it to be effective after the spawn when big bluegills are cautious. It also performs well in clear water where the larger, noisier cork and deer-hair bugs fail.

Many otherwise proficient fly-fishers ignore the usefulness of standard dry flies. They are thought to be tools of the trout fisher, but large bluegills, after the spawn, can be as selective as any fish that swims. It is equally productive to "match the hatch" for *Lepomis macrochirus.* Lacking that, here are some dry-fly patterns that have been successful for us in a variety of situations.

Adams

Hook: Mustad 94840 (barbed) or 94845 (barbless), size 10-16
Tail: Mixed grizzly and brown hackle
Body: Gray muskrat fur
Wings: Grizzly hackle tips tied upright
Hackle: Mixed grizzly and brown, or cree, cape
Head: Gray thread

Note: The Adams was originally tied for trout, and is one of those flies that is designed to imitate the mayfly form. It is particularly valuable in streams, but shouldn't be overlooked in still waters.

Black Gnat

Hook: Mustad 94840 or 94845, size 10-16
Tail: Red hackle fibers
Body: Peacock herl
Wings: Gray mallard wing feather sections
Hackle: Black cape
Head: Black thread

Note: Again, this pattern imitates nothing in particular, but has been very effective for us when fished at the edges of willows or near emergent vegetation. It holds a special place in our hearts as the first pattern to take a fly rod-caught bluegill for us decades ago.

Mosquito

Hook: Mustad 94840 or 94845, size 10-16
Tail: Grizzly hackle fibers
Body: One dark and one light strand of moose mane wound together
Wing: Grizzly hackle tips
Hackle: Grizzly cape
Head: Gray thread

Note: Summer evenings can produce vicious mosquito hatches on many bluegill ponds. When you start to feel bites, tie on the mosquito pattern right before you apply the insect repellent.

Renegade

Hook: Mustad 94840 or 94845, size 10-16
Tag: Flat gold tinsel
Rear Hackle: Brown cape
Body: Peacock herl
Front Hackle: White neck
Head: Olive thread

Note: This is another fly developed for trout that appears just as succulent to surface-feeding bream. It's fore and aft hackles make it a particularly good floater. We use it frequently in low-light conditions because the white hackle remains visible to us.

McGinty

Hook: Mustad 94840 or 94845, size 10-12
Tail: Barred teal over red hackle fibers
Body: Yellow and black chenille wound alternately and divided
Hackle: Dark brown hen hackle
Wings: White-tipped mallard sections tied upright

Note: The McGinty pattern represents a bumblebee, and is an especially effective summer pattern. Most fish have a sense of taste, but the theory that the venom-producing acid glands in bees may enhance the fish's satisfaction from consuming this insect is debatable. It is more likely that bluegills easily recognize bees as food. In fact, this has proven to be an effective pattern for us when fished in the shade on sunny and hot summer mid-afternoons—times that would otherwise be considered quite slow. McGintys may be fished wet or dry.

Floater/Divers

The only available pattern specifically designed for bluegills which floats at rest and dives upon retrieve is Jack Ellis's Fathead Diver. This fly appears to the fish as something disabled which is trying desperately to escape. Often the fish cannot resist this easy morsel.

Fathead Diver

Hook: Straight eye, standard wire, size 10
Wing: Short gray squirrel tail over which is red followed by brown marabou
Head and Collar: Natural deer-body hair spun and trimmed like a Dahlberg Diver and well-cemented on the collar, lightly cemented on the head

Note: Jack Ellis also incorporates a monofilament weed guard which he forms with a slightly larger loop. Tighter loops tend to become "fishless" rather than weedless because monofilament is simply too stiff to give with the strikes. The pattern we've given is the original. We've had good success with all-black, all-olive, and all-white Fathead Divers.

Wet Flies

As their name implies, wet flies are designed to be fished beneath the surface of the water. Some sink simply because there is nothing buoyant to keep them afloat. Others incorporate materials that absorb water and, therefore, become naturally weighted while some have weighting material tied into the body of the fly. We use three different types of wet patterns in our fishing—standard wets, soft-hackle flies, and a category we call bream killers.

With one exception, the standard wet flies we use are old trout patterns that bluegill anglers have adopted. The one exception is a great pattern created by master angler and author, Tom Nixon, whose *Fly Tying and Fly Fishing for Bass and Panfish* was written in 1968 (A. S. Barnes & Co. Inc., Cranbury, New Jersey). The fly is called the Cajun Coachman.

Cajun Coachman

Hook: Mustad 9672, sizes 6-12
Underbody: Eight to ten turns of .025 lead wire
Body: Back half: Red floss tied well down the hook bend (originally, Tom tied this as a red tag, but has modified it) Front half: Peacock herl
Throat: Brown hackle fibers
Wing: A single broad black-and-white barred wood duck flank feather folded in half lengthwise before being tied in

Note: Tom Nixon tied this pattern to be fished in the bayous and marshes of Louisiana, but we've found it to be a real fish-getter in other waters as well. It is an exceptionally heavy fly that gets deep in a hurry, and must be cast with an open loop. The Cajun Coachman works best for us when retrieved in slow two-inch strips or when using a slow hand-twist retrieve.

Woolly Worm (White)

Hook: Mustad 3906, size 6-8
Tail: Short red marabou fibers
Underbody: Six to eight turns of .025 lead wire
Body: White chenille
Hackle: White, palmered
Head: White thread

Note: This is another heavy pattern that requires an open loop to be cast effectively. Of course, it can be tied in other colors, but we've enjoyed particular success with this pattern. It is a favorite of bluegill expert Lou Vogele of Fayetteville, Arkansas. This pattern is effective throughout the season and, because of its size and weight, it's particularly good at taking larger fish. It should be counted down and retrieved very slowly.

Orange Fish Hawk

Hook: Mustad 3906, size 8-14
Tail: None
Body: Orange floss
Hackle: Soft grizzly hackle, tied oversized and sparse

Note: This simple pattern is unweighted and sinks tantalizingly to tempt fish that might pass up a fly which falls more rapidly. We've had success with the Orange Fish Hawk when fished in the shade in midsummer. While it can be tied with other body colors, this one has produced best for us.

Grizzly King

Hook: Mustad 3906 or equivalent, size 8-14
Tail: Strip of red duck quill
Body: Green floss ribbed with gold tinsel
Hackle: Grizzly
Wings: Gray mallard side feather fibers
Head: Black thread

Professor

Hook: Mustad 3906 or equivalent, sizes 8-14
Tail: Red hackle fibers
Body: Yellow silk floss ribbed with flat gold tinsel
Hackle: Dark ginger
Wings: Speckled gray mallard flank

Note: These last two flies are old trout patterns that have proven effective for bluegills. Tied in smaller sizes, we've had our greatest success with them in small, slow-moving streams and they are at their best in late summer and early fall.

Soft-hackle Flies

Soft-hackle flies date back to the second century A.D. They consist only of a floss or dubbed body and sparsely wound breast or flank feather from a partridge, quail, grouse, woodcock, or starling.

The popularity of these flies was rejuvenated by Sylvester Nemes in *The Soft-Hackled Fly* (©1975, The Chatham Press, Old Greenwich, Connecticut). Trout-chasers attribute soft hackles' success to their impressionistic imitation of emerging caddisflies. Their ease

More big bluegills will locate near submerged wood structure than anywhere else in the pond.
Lefty Wilson photo

This eleven-inch bluegill (shown actual size) was released to thrill another angler.

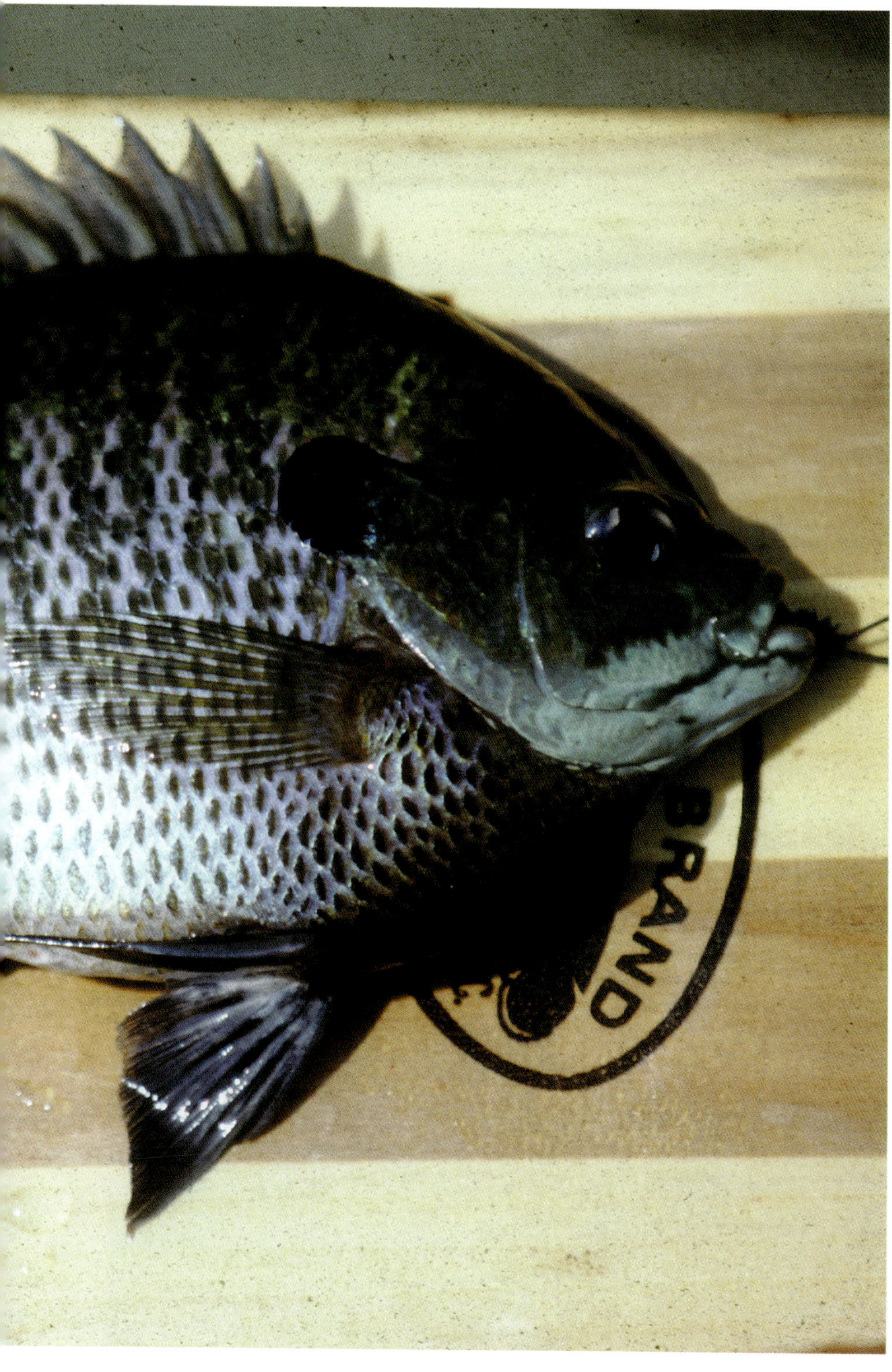
BRAND

Small cork poppers have been traditional fare for bluegills since the late nineteenth century.

Docks with additional cover and access to deep water can be unbeatable.

Light rods and big bluegills are an irresistible combination.

Delicate presentations are most productive for wary, shade-hugging bluegills. *Lefty Wilson photo*

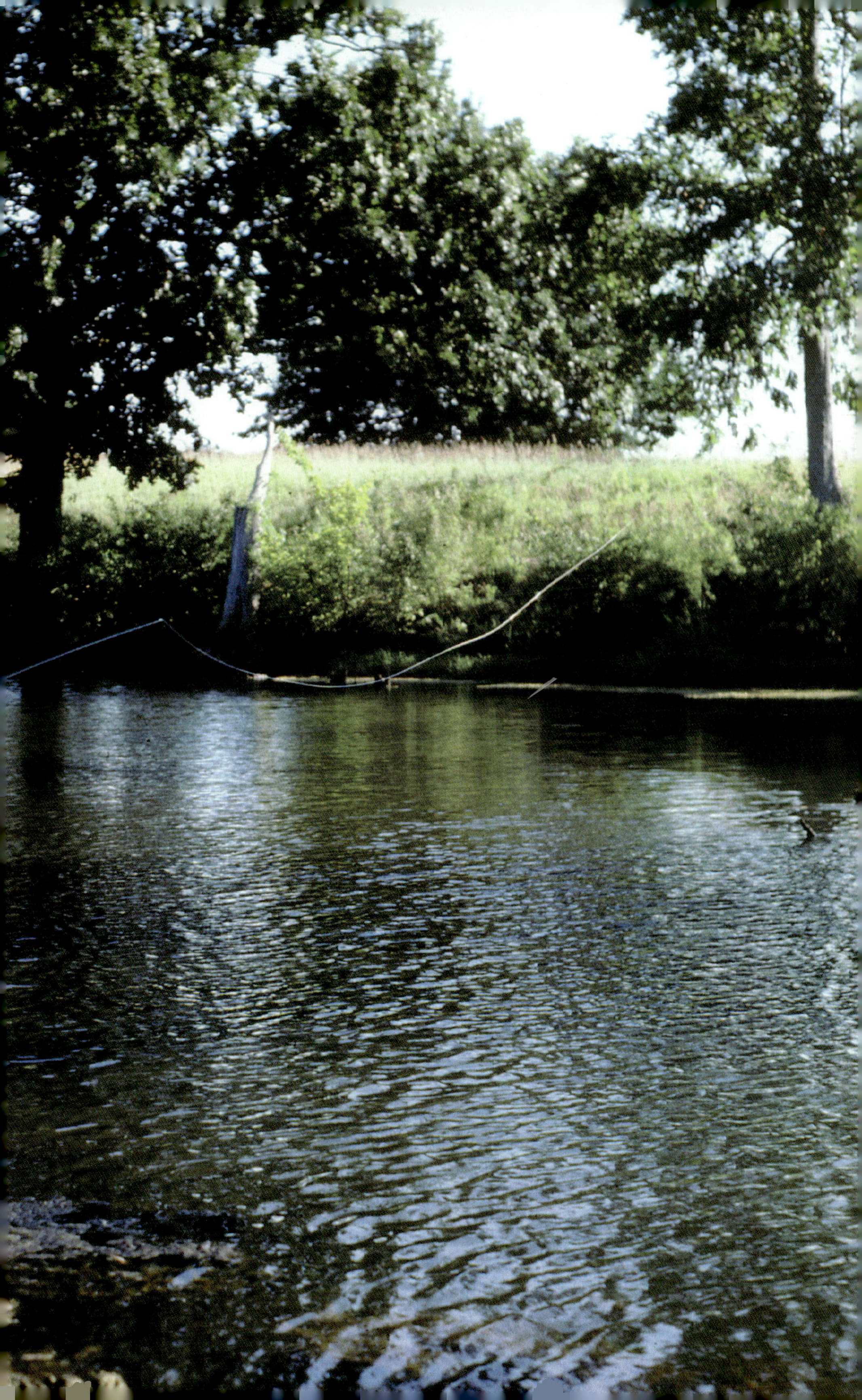

A handful of pure pugnacity.

Shaded coves provide good action in the heat of summer.

When the water first warms, there are great opportunities for bluegill fishing.

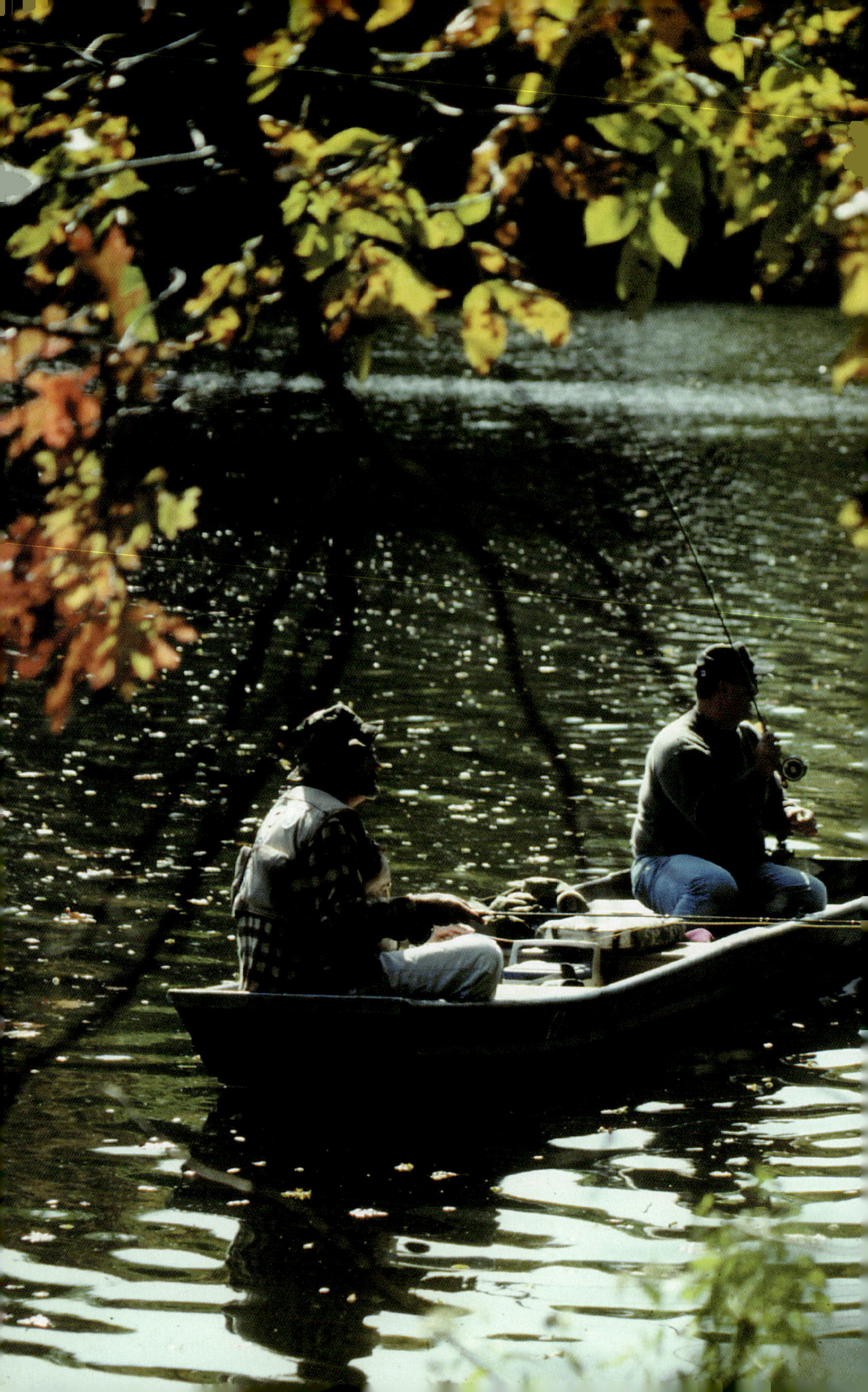

Good friends and great sport on a crisp autumn afternoon.

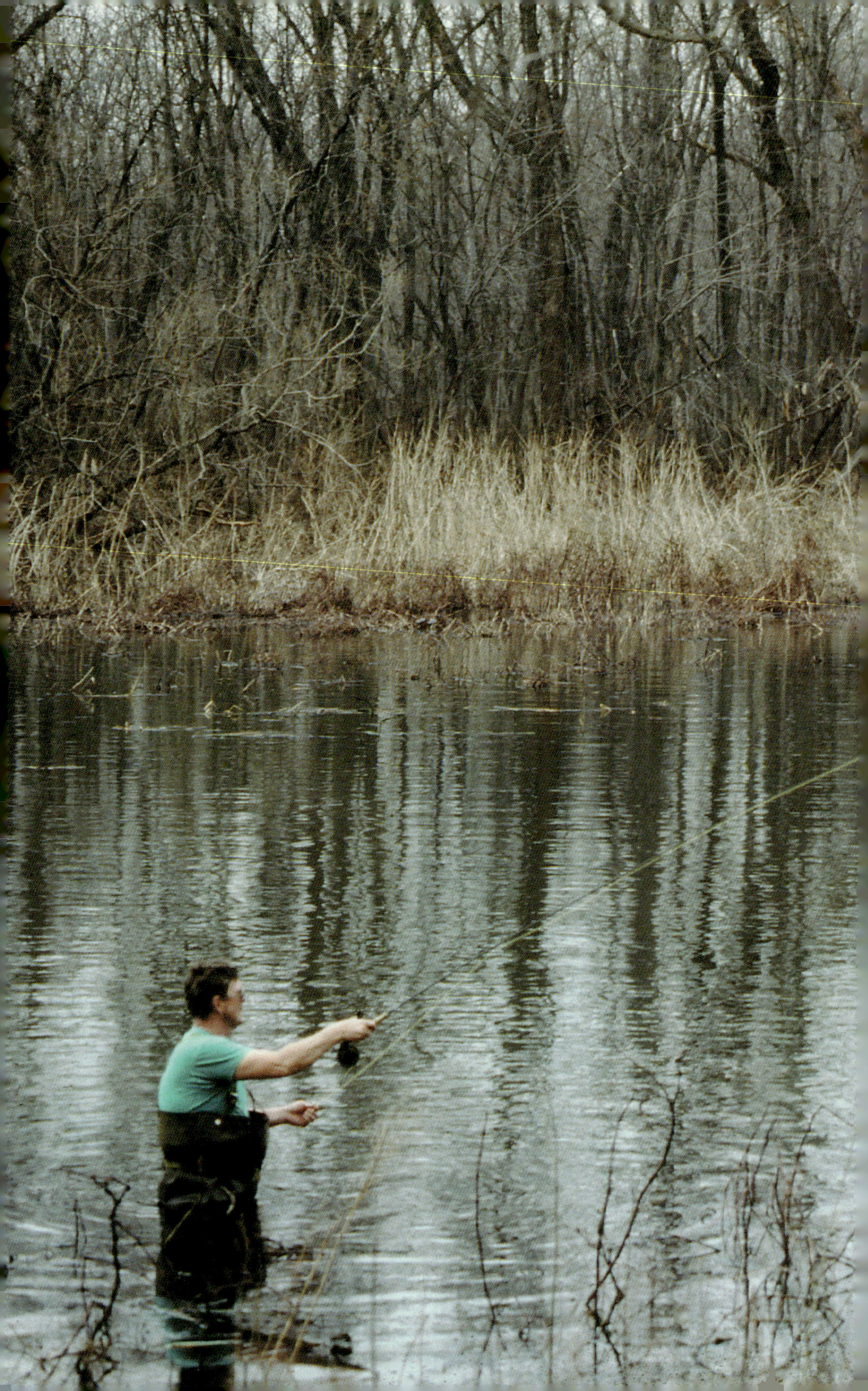

Oxbow lakes like this one along the Illinois River can provide great late-season fishing and solitude.

Dry Flies

Bully's Bluegill Spider **Adams** **Black Gnat**

Renegade **McGinty** **Mosquito**

Floaters/Divers

Fathead Diver (white) **Fathead Diver (black)**

Wet & Soft-Hackle Flies

Cajun Coachman **Woolly Worm (white)** **Orange Fish Hawk**

Grizzly King **Professor** **Soft Hackle**

Bream Killers

Gill Getter **Hum Bug** **Yuk Bug**

NYMPHS

North Fork Nymph **Whitlock's Damselfly Nymph (olive)** **Tellico Nymph**

Scud (olive) **Gold Ribbed Hare's Ear Nymph** **Oscar's *Hexagenia* Nymph**

STREAMERS

Black Nose Dace (Thunder Creek style) **Black Ghost Marabou**

Mickey Finn **Woolly Bugger (olive)** **Thender Spin (white)**

TERRESTRIALS

Catalpa Worm **Letort Cricket** **Foam Beetle** **Caterpillar**

WORMS & CRAYFISH

San Juan Worm **Galyardt's Foxy Crayfish**

JIM SCHOLLMEYER

The color of bluegills varies depending on the time of year and the water in which they live.

of tying recommends them for fishing brushy areas which may consume several. Losing complex ties in these areas can be aggravating.

Hook: Mustad 94840 or 94845, sizes 6-14
Body: Green UNI-Stretch thread (orange and pink work well, too)
Ribbing: Copper wire
Hackle: Partridge hackle tied sparsely
Head: Black thread

Bream Killers

"Bream Killers," by our definition, are sinking flies small enough for bluegills which incorporate rubber hackle into the pattern. It is our general description for a large number of regional favorites that seem to defy other classification. By definition, then, our own Bully's Bluegill Spider is a bream killer. Others that have proven successful for us include the Gill Getter, Hum Bug, and Yuk Bug.

Gill Getter

Hook: Mustad 3906, size 6-12
Underbody: Six to eight wraps of .020 lead wire
Tail: Moose mane
Legs: White rubber hackle
Body: Fluorescent green chenille
Shellback: Moose mane that is the continuation of mane used for the tail
Head: Fluorescent green thread

Note: The Gill Getter first came to our attention in the pages of *Flies for Bass and Panfish* (c1992, Northland Press, Inc.) by Dick Stewart and Farrow Allen. It is attributed to Tom Lentz and is designed to be fished deeply along concrete pilings and steep drop-offs.

Hum Bug

Hook: Straight eye, standard wire, sizes 6-12
Body: Yellow chenille
Legs: White rubber hackle
Back: Black chenille
Head: Black thread

Note: This unweighted pattern is fished in the shallows where a slow fall and retrieve enhance its attractiveness.

Yuk Bug

Hook: Down eye, 4X long, size 6-10
Underbody: Ten turns of .025 lead wire
Tail: Gray squirrel tail
Body: Black chenille
Legs: Three white rubber hackle legs evenly spaced along each side of the body, slanting back
Hackle: Light badger, palmered
Head: Black thread

Note: This heavy pattern, understandably classified as a nymph by many, requires casting care. When retrieved slowly along rocky ledges, it is a good producer. It was originally tied for Western trout, and is one of several patterns adaptable to the bluegill-fisherman's needs.

Nymphs

Nymphs, which are immature aquatic insects, rank very high on the bluegill's list of favorite foods. It is certainly productive to match the nymph to the locale you are fishing, but larvae are difficult to find in still waters with muddy bottoms and lots of vegetation. It is most easily accomplished by observing and capturing the hatched adult insects and then researching their nymphal forms. A good source for this work is Ernest Schwiebert's *Nymphs* (c1973, Winchester Press, Tulsa, Oklahoma). Armed with this information, accurate nymph patterns can be purchased or tied to represent those in your pond or lake.

In moving waters, it is usually a much easier process. You need only turn over a few stream-bottom rocks to discover the nymphs themselves. However their identity is discovered, they will be readily accepted by the bluegills if tied and fished properly.

Some will be most effective when crawled slowly along the bottom. We have had excellent results by allowing our nymphs to sink all the way to the bottom and then gently and smoothly lifting the rod tip two or three feet into the air. This causes your fly to appear to swim toward the surface where a real nymph would shed its nymphal husk and become an airborne adult. Nymphs are particularly vulnerable at this time, and bluegills capitalize by feeding voraciously on them. This technique is most effective during a hatch, and is always satisfying to the angler because it requires identification, proper matching, and skillful presentation to catch the larger fish.

Here are several nymph patterns we've used successfully in a variety of water types:

North Fork Nymph

Hook: Mustad 9672, sizes 10-16
Tail: Pheasant tail fibers
Abdomen: Same pheasant tail fibers wrapped around thread and wound around hook shank
Thorax Underbody: Five to six turns of .020 lead wire (optional)
Thorax: Natural rabbit-fur dubbing, original color
Legs: Pick out guard hairs from thorax
Head: Black thread

Note: This general representation of a mayfly nymph is our version of the old Pheasant Tail Nymph tied by legendary English river keeper, Frank Sawyer, long ago. It is designed to match the nymphs we found crawling around the bottom of southern Missouri's North Fork River. Originally tied for trout, we soon discovered its appeal to the bluegills, too.

Whitlock's Damselfly Nymph (Olive)

Hook: Mustad 9672, sizes 8-10
Eyes: 2.5 mm black strung pearls or melted monofilament
Tail: Olive grizzly marabou
Rib: Copper wire
Thorax: Olive fur
Legs: Olive grouse or partridge
Wing Case: Olive Swiss straw
Head: Olive thread

Note: Damselfly nymphs are readily available as a year-round food source in most bluegill waters. They inhabit subaquatic vegetation making them available and vulnerable to bluegills. There are several patterns available. This accurate representation was originated by Dave Whitlock, whose contribution to warmwater fly fishing is well known.

Tellico Nymph

Hook: Mustad 3906, sizes 8-14
Tail: Soft, brown hackle fibers
Shellback: Pheasant tail fibers
Body: Yellow wool or floss tied very full
Rib: Peacock herl
Legs: 3 or 4 turns of soft brown hackle

Note: It is hard to imagine what this old Smoky Mountain pattern represents, but bluegills agree that it looks good enough to eat. It seems to work best as an attractor on bright, sunny days.

Scud (Olive)

Hook: Down eye, 1X long, humped, sizes 8-12
Tail: Olive hen hackle fibers
Body: Dark olive rabbit dubbing
Shellback: Clear plastic
Rib: Gold wire
Legs: Picked out guard hairs
Head: Olive thread or brass bead

Note: Scuds (freshwater shrimp) inhabit many freshwater ponds and streams and are an abundant and prized portion of the bluegill's diet. Recently we have used this pattern tied as a bead-head with great results.

Gold Ribbed Hare's Ear Nymph

Hook: Mustad 9672, sizes 10-16
Tail: Hare's mask fur with guard hairs
Abdomen: Hare's mask fur with guard hairs
Rib: Oval gold tinsel
Thorax: Hare's mask fur with guard hairs, tied thick
Wing Case: Goose wing quill segment
Legs: Fur from the thorax picked out

Note: This is a popular pattern for trout and smallmouth, and is equally effective for bluegills.

Oscar's Hexagenia Nymph

Hook: Mustad 9575, sizes 8-12
Tail: Short, soft, brown hackle and three to four ring-necked pheasant tail barbs
Underbody: Dental floss built into a tapered body and flattened with pliers
Abdomen: Cream sparkle yarn
Rib: Oval gold tinsel
Abdomen Top: Pheasant tail or mottled turkey, lacquered
Gills: A gray stem of down from a partridge or pheasant, trimmed and folded over the top of the abdomen before pulling the turkey or pheasant tail over
Thorax: Orange sparkle yarn
Hackle: Brown hackle palmered over the thorax and trimmed across the bottom
Wing Case: Lacquered pheasant tail or mottled turkey
Head and Eyes: Orange thread around fifteen-pound-test melted monofilament eyes

Note: Southern ponds with mud bottoms have lots of *Hexagenia limbata* mayflies which begin hatching at dark. Rather than match sometimes sparse hatches with dries, try this nymph pattern credited to Oscar Feliu in *Flies For Bass and Panfish* (c1992, Northland Press, Inc., Intervale, NH).

Streamers

Streamers are designed to imitate small baitfish. They are often ignored by bluegill fishermen, and this is a mistake. Bluegills are avid minnow feeders and, like most other species, will even attack their own fry.

Recently, there have been some excellent new streamers designed to represent nearly any finny water creature, and some work perfectly well. Occasionally, however, gifted tiers create beautiful and complex patterns without regard to their practical function. Any fly too costly or intricate to be tossed into heavy cover has little value except as an ornament. Our preferences in streamers, therefore, are simple and basic.

Black Nose Dace (Thunder Creek Style)

Hook: 4-6X long, down eye, size 6-12
Thread: Red
Body: Flat silver or Mylar tinsel
Lateral Stripe: Black bucktail
Back: Brown bucktail
Belly: White bucktail
Eye: Yellow lacquer with black dot

Note: This bass-fry imitation works well from late spring through summer when fished around protective cover.

Black Ghost Marabou

Hook: 4-6X long, down eye, size 6-12
Tail: Yellow hackle fibers
Body: Black floss
Rib: Flat silver tinsel
Beard: Yellow hackle fibers
Wing: White marabou
Head: Black thread
Cheek: Jungle cock (optional)

Mickey Finn

Hook: Mustad 9575, size 10
Body: Silver Mylar tubing secured in back with red tying thread
Wing: Sparse bunch of yellow bucktail over an equal bunch of red bucktail over a larger bunch of yellow bucktail
Head: Black thread

Note: An old fly that is a good attractor pattern for trout works just as well for bream.

Woolly Bugger (Olive)

Hook: Mustad 9672, sizes 6-12
Tail: Light olive marabou; with several strands of Krystal Flash (optional)
Body: Peacock herl
Hackle: Grizzly, palmered
Head: Olive thread

Note: Although it has only been around since the late 1970s, this fly has become so popular it is regarded as a classic. It can be fished as a streamer, a large nymph or a leech. Whatever it is mistaken for, it belongs in every fly-fisher's box, and bluegill fishermen are no exception. In slow-moving waters, Woolly Buggers are especially effective when drifted in front of undercut banks, then stopped and twitched. We have a friend who fishes them almost exclusively with excellent results.

Thunder Spin (White)

Hook: Mustad 9672, size 4-8
Wing and Head: White marabou tied Thunder Creek style
Gills: One wrap of red chenille
Trailer: Small round spinner added by slipping over the hook barb which must be left in place

Note: This exceptionally large pattern was created by Kentucky Lake guide and fly rod lure innovator, Ron Kruger. It was originally tied for fishing the shad bursts when white bass slash through huge schools of threadfin shad. It is surprisingly efficient for monster bluegills as well. It casts remarkably well considering its bulk, sinks at a tantalizing rate with constant flashes, and tends to stay at the same level the retrieve is initiated.

We weight all of our streamers so they can be fished deeply along the weed edges or in the tops of submerged trees and brush. It is also important to keep the bulkiness associated with many streamers to a minimum. Remember that bluegills love minnows but have small mouths.

Terrestrials

Any land-based insect which might inadvertently fall or be blown into the water qualifies as a terrestrial. The list of possibilities is long and geographically diverse. Here are several fly dressings that have done well for us and merit your consideration:

Catalpa Worm

Hook: Down eye, 4X long, slightly humped, sizes 8-10
Tail: Black goose biots
Body: Cream or pale-yellow wool
Back: Black chenille along the top like a shellback
Hackle: Black, stripped on one side, palmered, then clipped short

Note: Jack Ellis's pattern represents one of the many leaf-eating worms that bluegills savor. Fish this pattern under overhanging tree branches and be prepared for jolting strikes.

Letort Cricket

Hook: Down eye, 2XL, sizes 8-10
Body: Black fur
Wing: Black wing quill tied flat over the body
Head: Black deer body hair spun and trimmed to shape

Note: Floating cricket patterns are most effectively fished on warm evenings when the naturals are stirring. Ed Shenk created this fly for trout in the limestone streams near his Pennsylvania home.

Foam Beetle

Hook: Mustad 94840, sizes 10-12
Body: Peacock herl
Legs: Starling hackle, tied sparsely
Shellback and Head: Black closed-cell foam strip pulled forward and tied off with red thread leaving a protrusion of foam for the head

Note: Nearly indestructible and unsinkable, the Foam Beetle is a terrific pattern for late summer near logs, docks, and tree branches.

Caterpillar

Hook: Down eye, 6X long, sizes 6-10
Body: Natural deer body hair spun and clipped into a cylindrical shape
Hackle: Grizzly, palmered over the deer hair

Note: This is a Tom Nixon design to be fished under overhanging tree branches. Colors and sizes may be matched to the naturals found in your area.

Others

Three flies we use in specific situations just don't seem to fit any of the other six categories. Worm imitations are useful in any water. We use them when fishing post-spawn bluegills off drop-offs and over submerged humps. Crayfish are most effective for us in rock-lined waters where vegetation is sparse. Micro jigs can be easily tied to suit your needs and are best fished in heavy cover.

Worms

There is hardly an American child or adult interested in fishing who hasn't dangled an earthworm or red wiggler beneath a bobber in pursuit of bluegills. The reason is quite simple—they catch bluegills.

Have you ever wondered why? Earthworms are not regularly found in the fish's environment. Chuck Tryon, Missouri's trout guru, (*Fly Fishing for Trout in Missouri,* c1985, Ozark Mountain Fly-fishers, Rolla, MO) and fly expert (*Figuring Out Flies,* c1990, Ozark Mountain Fly-fishers) provides an answer.

"Few anglers know that nightcrawlers and earthworms have a common aquatic cousin called an oligochaete (oh-lih-go-keet). Except that they're often a brighter shade of red and seldom are as big as a nightcrawler, they're visually similar in every respect to their landbound kin."

Many fish, then, regularly see and feed on these creatures, and likely accept the land-based versions as oligochaetes. Despite the obvious advantage of their use, most fly-casters have largely ignored worm imitations.

San Juan Worm

Hook: 3-4X long, sizes 10-12
Thread: 06 red
Body: Red ultra-chenille strand along the hook shank and extending an inch or so both fore and aft
Rib: Fine copper wire, palmered

Note: This simple tie belongs in every bluegill fisher's fly box. Originally, the San Juan Worm was tied in size 20 or smaller using lengths of gold-ribbed red floss shorter than the hook shank. Use only ultra-chenille for the above pattern to prevent the ends from unraveling. Fish it very slowly and impart an occasional twitch to activate the dangling ends.

Crayfish

Like worms, crayfish are favorites of all game fish. Trotline fishermen bait their hooks with them, bait-casters pitch them, and, unlike worm imitations, fly tiers duplicate them with countless patterns. Some are simple and impressionistic. Others are intricate, realistic models designed more to display the tier's artistic skills than to catch fish.

The bluegill angler primarily needs to consider fly size in creating patterns. This means duplicating the younger crayfish that are nearly translucent because they have not yet formed their hardened shells. Over the years, we have been frustrated in finding a pattern of appropriate size that not only fishes well, but also is durable. We tried to create our own, without success, before we were introduced to the solution by fly tier, Dennis Galyardt. Dennis is the warmwater editor of the Federation of Fly-fishers' publication, *The Fly-fisher*.

Galyardt's Foxy Crayfish

Hook: 2XL, down-eye, sizes 6-10
Antennae: Rust deer body hair and two strands of orange Krystal Flash
Eyes: Small lead barbell eyes
Pinchers and Legs: Clump of red fox fur
Thorax and Abdomen: Red fox under-fur dubbing
Carapace or Shell: Tan Furry Foam touched with brown magic marker
Rib: Fine copper wire

Note: Like any crayfish pattern, this one must be weighted to be effective because crayfish crawl along the bottoms of lakes and streams. As a result, these flies may become entangled in the weeds and moss found in most good bluegill water.

Dennis offers the following advice, "I often fish this pattern under a strike indicator, suspending it near vertical cover, rock bluffs or over weed beds. In moving water, I fish it without a retrieve because tiny crayfish are often at the mercy of the current and are poor swimmers."

Micro Jigs

Tiny jigs with weighted heads of 1/64 to 1/124 ounces can be irresistible to big bluegills. They offer several advantages to conventionally tied flies. Because the heads contain all the weight, they drop more vertically in a head-down, hook-up position. They can be dropped directly into the thickest cover and are less likely to snag branches and vegetation. Micro jigs also are easily retrieved with a hopping or undulating action.

Any fly pattern in any color combination can be tied as a micro jig, but hook size is an important consideration in their construction. One particularly avid micro jig enthusiast, Dennis Galyardt, has some good advice for micro jig practitioners: "I prefer size-10 gold hooks on my jigs. Since I always fish near brush and weeds, the life expectancy of flies is pretty short. Gold hooks are a little softer, and bend before the leader snaps."

Dennis also recommends using heavy leaders: "I will use a leader that tests around four pounds. Under tougher conditions with brush and weeds . . . I often increase the tippet to 10-pound test."

Chapter 5
CHOOSING THE RIGHT WATER

"AT BEST THE LAKES AND STREAMS ARE MIRRORS REFLECTING THE SURROUNDING SCENERY. FOR THE ALERT FISHERMAN, ESPECIALLY THE FLY-FISHERMAN, THE SURFACE IS NOT A MIRROR BUT A WINDOW."

Paul Schullery
Home Waters
Gary Soucie, Ed.
©1991, Fireside Books
New York, New York

Choosing the Right Water

The most critical element of the fishing puzzle is selecting the right water. We can choose the best equipment and make the perfect presentation, but if both are used in the wrong water, the odds of success are longer than winning a lottery jackpot. Many lakes are incapable of sustaining bluegills, and much of the remaining water cannot produce the numbers and size we're after. By fishing only in water capable of producing good fish, we can improve our odds tremendously.

Few anglers do this. Most fish randomly selected water, relying solely on luck. Often, they are fishing water that produces either very few fish or, more likely, a bluegill-population explosion of badly stunted fish.

On rare occasions, someone will catch a large bluegill from one of these lakes, and word will spread about the catch and the angler's remarkable skill. The assumption is that there are many big bluegills there, but that only gifted fishermen can fool them. The lucky fisherman, of course, does nothing to dissuade people from thinking that he is indeed a master angler, but he is always very secretive about his methods.

The truth is, by understanding different water types, knowing the requirements of bluegills, and by making adjustments based on seasonal and daily changes, we can eliminate most of the unproductive water. This will enable us to be successful a much higher percentage of the time.

There are three basic types of bluegill-producing water—natural lakes, impounded lakes, and moving water. No matter where water is located, it undergoes seasonal, annual, and multi-year changes. In remote areas, multi-year changes may be so subtle they cannot be recognized in a lifetime. Changes elsewhere may be relatively obvious. Successful anglers must understand and recognize how these changes affect the water and the bluegills they intend to fish.

In lakes, long-term changes occur from an aging process called eutrophication. In simplified form, every lake will eventually fill with sediment and/or organic detritus, get progressively shallower and finally become dry land. This is a natural process, usually taking centuries, even millennia, but intervention by man often accelerates the process dramatically.

Each body of water is distinctly different. Each has its own nutrient chemistry, bottom material and structure, plant life and aquatic life, including fish.

Natural Lakes

Like all living organisms, each body of water is constantly changing. "Young" lakes are deep and clear with little or no vegetation, while older ones are shallow, murky, and produce abundant weed growth. Vegetative abundance is due in part to the water's mineral richness and, in general, the more plant life a body of water produces, the larger the fish population it can support.

Many natural lakes were formed when the last ice age receded from the northern United States. Although spring runoff may raise the level of these lakes, summer levels remain fairly constant. From a fishing standpoint, this means that fish movements are more predictable than in waters that fluctuate widely. Fishermen can locate the fish in natural lakes more consistently, and the fish will remain in more predictable patterns throughout the season.

Here, the key structural element for bluegills is the weedline along the lake's shallow perimeter and on off-shore humps or submerged islands. This is true through all seasons of the year, including the winter season when weeds are decomposing. In natural lakes, bluegills are shallow in the weeds, or deep in the weeds, or somewhere in between. Within this relatively narrow area, bluegills will move on a seasonal and daily basis, depending on their needs and constantly changing conditions.

One major exception to the weedline-location rule is when schools of bluegills suspend over deep water with little cover. This occurs when predator species dominate the lake and force the bluegills out of shallow areas. Another exception is when a prolific hatch induces them to cruise at the surface over open water in large schools of voracious feeders. We suspect they are feeding on emerging insects, possibly Chironomids or midges. We'll discuss this more in Chapter 7.

Weedline depth is determined by sunlight penetration. We prefer water that is somewhat discolored, thereby preventing deep weed growth. This forces bluegills to use areas that are more shallow, which enables a much more simplified and pleasing presentation of our flies. It also requires bluegills to live in closer proximity to one another instead of scattering over a larger area.

If sunlight penetrates deeply enough to enable weeds to grow at a depth of twenty feet, available cover will not only be that deep, but also extend much further from shore. The weed-covered area, then, will be enormous and, while it may well produce a greater number of fish than a shallow weed line, they will be much more difficult to locate.

Our ideal natural lake would be moderately fertile, with murky water, floating microscopic algae and abundant weed growth. It would contain a healthy adult population of predators such as largemouth bass and would be managed to maintain this balance.

A natural fishery of this quality is the exception rather than the rule, which points out the importance of choosing your fishery with care. Not many anglers are able to consistently fish the ideal setting. This does not mean that a quality fishing experience on lesser water isn't possible, but simply that infertile water and stunted populations can lead to frustrating fishing experiences.

Impoundments

Impounded waters, relatively new to the fishing scene, are a whole new ball game. At the turn of the century, only 100 impoundments larger than five-hundred acres had been created in the United States. Slowly, over the next four decades, the number increased to more than 1,500 of these relatively large man-made lakes.

During the same period, millions of smaller impoundments have also been created. Texas alone has over one million. All of these reservoirs were made for a wide variety of purposes, including hydroelectric power, irrigation, flood control, and livestock watering. Not many were made with recreational uses in mind, yet they have produced great fishing opportunities for millions of people where few, if any, existed before.

Impounded waters are not all alike. They vary dramatically from extremely deep, infertile waters created by damming rivers which flow through steep-sided canyons to shallow, vegetation-choked lakes formed in agricultural regions. They are as different as the inundated lands they cover and their watersheds. Not all are capable of producing and sustaining bluegills, and significant numbers have only marginal fisheries.

A System For Recognizing Bluegill Factories

Despite these vast differences, it is relatively simple to recognize the "bluegill factories" among them, and to pick out the lake sections most likely to provide the best bluegill fishing. To assist fly-fishers in recognizing these productive waters, we have identified eight characteristics the best bluegill waters share. Some lake characteristics are inter-related, but in all cases they are either recognizable upon inspection or easily researched.

Not all good bluegill water will possess all eight characteristics, but the more of these characteristics the water has, the more large bluegills are likely to be produced. While we have treated natural lakes as a separate entity, and will further discuss ponds and strip-mine pits later, we find this set of criteria universal in evaluating potential bluegill water of all types, including streams. In no particular order of importance, our eight criteria include:

1. Nutrient richness. Nutrients produce microscopic life which initiates the food chain ultimately enabling bluegills at all stages of life to have access to growth-producing sustenance. The more abundant the nutrients, the more food is produced.

A visual examination will quickly tell us what we need to know. Nutrient-rich water has suspended material in it and is, therefore, cloudy or murky as opposed to clear. The murkiness should not be confused with turbidity caused by suspended silt either washed into the water or the result of wind and wave action. Ideal bluegill water may be so clouded by microscopic algae that your fingertips are unseen with your hand immersed to the wrist.

Nutrient-rich water is created in one of three ways, according to Chuck Tryon, a retired wildland hydrologist, master fly-fisher and author. "Number one, the nutrient richness of the soil which drains to the lake or stream. Secondly, any man-made additions like agricultural fertilizers and municipal sewage, and finally, the age of the lake. Older lakes gradually accumulate a build-up of nutrients and, consequently, are more enriched."

All other factors being equal, the most nutrient-rich waters are found in agricultural areas and, so too, are most of the best bluegill waters. When asked to pick the very best area in the United States for producing large numbers of big bluegills, fly-tackle representative and fly-fisher, David Halblom of Des Moines, Iowa, answered, "I'd choose from a band that included northern and central Illinois extending across Iowa into Nebraska. I know that would surprise a lot of people, but water fertility is the key to big bluegills."

Big bluegills utilize the oxygen and more desirable water temperatures brought into the pond by the flow from inlet creeks.

2. Abundant shallow water. Shallow water produces more life in all forms than deep water. This is due primarily to three factors. Sunlight penetrates thin water to a much higher degree than deep water. Sunlight is necessary to produce weed growth and algae.

Under most conditions, this is the area which provides the living room, kitchen and dining room for bluegills. There is protective cover and food. The larger the shallow areas of any water, the better the bluegill fishing will be with all other factors being equal.

Yet despite the importance of shallow water, some relatively deep water is necessary in sections of the country where lakes and ponds freeze over. This is not true in the deep South were the danger of winterkill caused by oxygen depletion is unlikely. Dixie's bayous are an example of uniformly shallow water capable of producing large numbers of big bluegills.

3. Abundant vegetation. While aquatic plant growth is, to a large extent, the product of our first two criteria, it is a key ingredient to producing lots of large bluegills. Coontail, milfoil, hydrilla,

lily pads, bulrushes, or any of a wide variety of other vegetation can provide the habitat necessary for bluegills.

The value of the vegetation is multi-faceted. Initially, it provides the bluegill fry with a place to hide from predators, enabling more of them to reach maturity. We could nearly say that the more abundant the weeds, the better the chances of big bluegills being produced, but there is a point of diminishing returns. If the aquatic jungle is so dense it prevents predators from removing significant numbers of small bluegills, these prolific spawners will overpopulate. The result is a stunted bluegill population caused by intensive competition for the available food.

In addition to providing a nursery for bluegill fry, vegetation also provides a lifetime food source for the bluegills. Not only do they feed on vegetation to some extent, but insect life, crustaceans, and minnows use the weeds as well. This provides a smorgasbord of feeding opportunities and produces the well-oxygenated water that sustains all life. It is difficult to overstate the importance of vegetation.

Several years ago, we fished a well-managed central Missouri pond with an enormous population of large bluegills. The pond was also home to large numbers of largemouth bass and some huge catfish. Heavy weed growth ringed the pond. The owner insisted on the practice of catch and release, and the water quickly acquired blue-ribbon status as a quality fishery.

Three years ago, unusually harsh winter weather blanketed the pond with several inches of snow and ice, while three weeks of intense cloudiness virtually blocked sunlight from the weeds. The weeds died out completely and the large fish population and decomposing vegetation used up all the available oxygen. Suddenly this magnificent fishery transformed into a barren sea. Even a small spring's flow wasn't enough to save the pond.

With the spring thaw, the banks were lined with decomposing fish and the owner hauled off pickup truck loads of the rotting carcasses. Sometimes we hear fishermen cursing weeds, frustrated because their flies constantly hang up in them but we should never underestimate their importance. They are the bluegill's lifeblood.

4. Warm water temperatures. All other things being equal, the warmer the water stays for the longest period of time, the larger the bluegills will grow. There is, however, an upper limit to water-temperature suitability. Bluegills are most comfortable between sixty-five and eighty degrees, and sustaining life is very difficult above ninety degrees for prolonged periods. Ideal bluegill-growing waters are those which remain between sixty-five and eighty degrees for most of the year, providing the bluegills with the longest possible growing season.

   Without hesitation, bluegill fly-fishing expert Lou Vogele, a retired U.S. Fish and Wildlife Service biologist, chose the deep South as the best area in the United States for producing large numbers of big bluegills. "The deep South, probably in Florida somewhere, would be my choice," says Vogele, "They've simply got a longer growing season than we do here in Arkansas."

5. Presence of woody structure. Although bluegills undeniably utilize many kinds of structure, sixty-five years of combined fly-fishing experience persuade us they prefer woody structure to any other, and it matters not whether the wood is natural (tree branches, standing timber, deadfalls, stumps) or man-made (boat docks, piers, duck-blinds). Most large bluegills will be found using woody structure with multiple projections protruding into the water. A downed tree extending its many-tentacled branches from the shallows into deep water is a good example of the very best kind of woody cover. There is some scientific evidence to suggest that bluegills feel more comfortable with the protection of a "roof" over their heads.

   Woody cover in conjunction with weeds is even better. In viewing a lake, pond, or stream with abundant shallow weeds, search for woody structure opportunities. They are the magnets that attract the most big bluegills. If you find several that have suitable spawning depths, bottom composition, and wood extending into deeper water, you have found the closest thing to a guarantee that exists in all of fishing. Bluegills use wood structure during all seasons of the year.

6. Presence of an abundant predator species. Uncontrolled, bluegills readily overpopulate their habitat and become stunted. This persuaded conservationists of a generation ago to

encourage anglers to remove all bluegills caught, no matter how small the waters. It was bad advice.

Even intense angling pressure cannot control large numbers of small fish. It is more likely that the larger fish will be removed, thus accelerating the stunting problem. The policy convinced generations of bluegill fishermen to keep larger fish. The result has been that in many lakes, ponds, and streams bluegills never had the opportunity to grow to their maximum size potential.

We know better now. While man can't control the small-bluegill population, a large number of any predator species can. We need many eight- to fifteen-inch (and larger) largemouth bass to keep bluegills in check, thus allowing survivors to grow into those eight- to ten-inch (and beyond) fish we all prefer to catch.

To gain an understanding of the relative health of the bluegill population in your favorite lake, pond, or stream, talk to someone who fishes hard for bluegill predators. If the bass fishermen tell you they are catching few one- to two-pound fish and even fewer lunkers, your bluegill fishing is in trouble. Your best protection against such a disaster is to convince the bass angler and all his friends to release the bass. What's best for his future fishing is also best for yours.

7. Gently sloping banks. We all dream about fishing lovely water, and steep-sided lakes are very picturesque. Usually such lakes have too much deep shoreline water to provide the shallow environment conducive to excellent bluegill fishing. Even in lakes with generally high banks, our attention should be focused on the areas that gently slope. All other factors being equal, this will compress the bluegills into a smaller area and afford us an accentuated opportunity for fast action. Gradual shorelines will provide more shallow water, more sunlight penetration, and therefore increase the likelihood of vegetation. The increased cover and food are essential in producing more and larger bluegills.

8. Abundant coves. A lake or pond with many coves is preferable to a body of water of the same size and perfectly round. This, too, is largely a function of shallow water. The more shoreline per surface acre of water, the more shallow water and,

consequently, the more bluegills produced. In addition, the serpentine shape of the ideal water also creates many more bluegill-holding structural elements. More cove endings, more primary and secondary points, and more humps, ridges, and depressions over what is likely to have been an irregular section of land before inundation can only enhance the lake's attractiveness to bluegills.

Six of the eight criteria in our bluegill-water identification system can be evaluated visually. Water temperature is easily taken, of course, and the presence of an abundant predator species can be ascertained either in conversation with other fishermen or through your own observations as you fish.

This system, then, enables us to determine which water in our locale will be productive even before we fish it. It also enables us to easily locate the isolated areas of large impoundments that will produce bluegills. Big lakes often are intimidating to the uninitiated because it seems an endless task to explore them and find fish. Now we are no longer prevented from accessing these vast waters successfully.

Finally, this system gives us a reasonable chance to be successful on unfamiliar waters. You might be vacationing in another section of the country and have the opportunity to fish. Even if it's a lake you've never seen before, you can determine what its resident population probably is and pinpoint the best areas to fish.

Fisheries biologists tell us that the larger multi-use reservoirs aren't really best for producing large numbers of big bluegills, but remember that these scientists are speaking in terms of fish produced per surface acre of water. In that respect, many large impoundments have too much deep water devoid of vegetation to be classified as great bluegill water and lake levels often fluctuate so dramatically that aquatic vegetation is reduced. That doesn't mean, however, that we can't have quality fishing on big lakes.

Understanding how to evaluate both natural lakes and impoundments enables us to choose the very best of these waters and eliminate the rest. Even when fishing a body of water that doesn't really fit our description of the best, it is possible to have excellent fishing by finding the areas that most nearly conform to the eight criteria we've described. The overall population of the lake may be small but some isolated areas may attract large numbers of big fish.

Young Lake

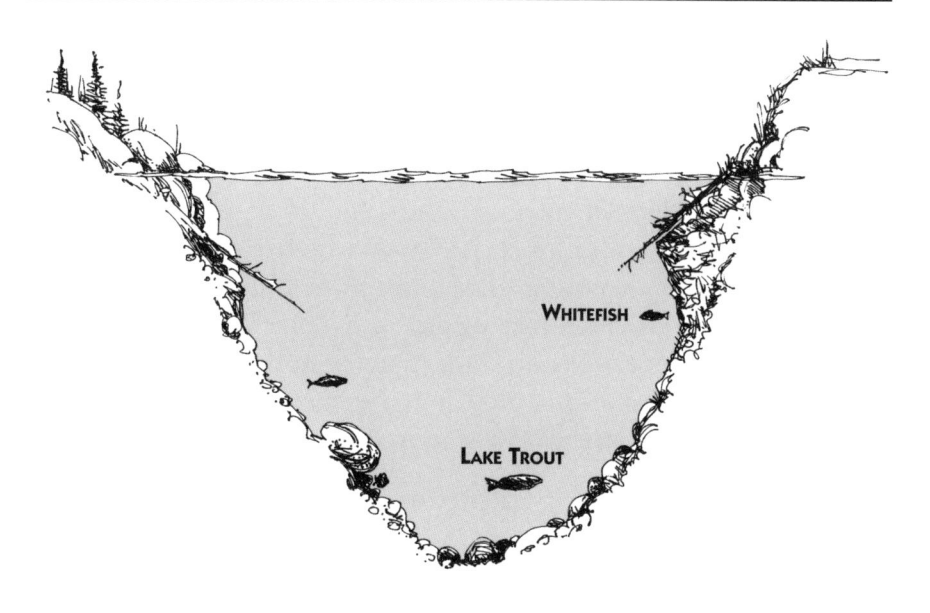

- Whitefish
- Lake Trout

Middle-Aged Lake

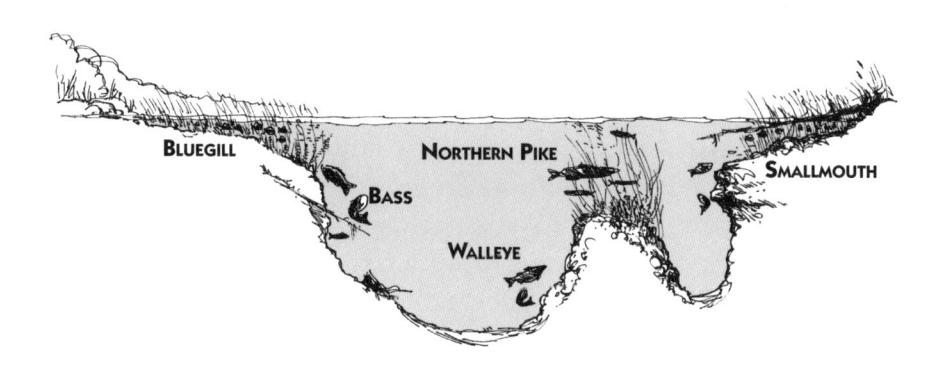

- Bluegill
- Bass
- Northern Pike
- Walleye
- Smallmouth

Old Lake

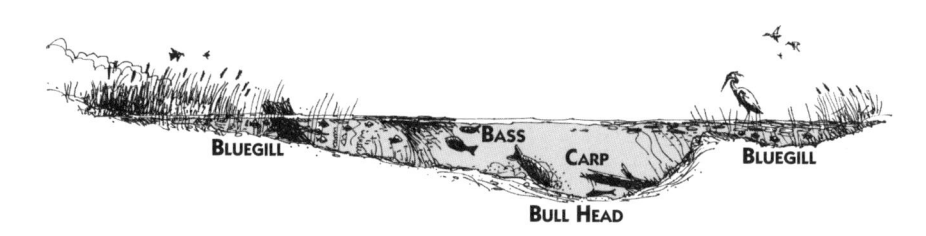

- Bluegill
- Bass
- Carp
- Bull Head
- Bluegill

Choosing the Right Water

Oxbow Lakes

Oxbows or backwater lakes are found in the flood plains of large rivers. They are replenished with water and fish when the nearby river floods. Most are murky, shallow, and have rich silt bottoms and abundant vegetation. They can provide excellent bluegill fishing from four key areas: 1. Still water at the sides of moving water, which may include inlet creeks, springs, and drain pipes that sometimes connect backwater lakes. 2. Flooded timber or deadfalls that provide overhead cover and attract desirable bluegill prey. 3. Old duck blinds that are often part of the backwater lake environment. They provide great cover and offer many feeding opportunities. 4. Uniformly shallow bottoms that may be successfully drift-fished (see Chapter 9) for scattered bluegills in the summer season.

Ponds

Ponds are merely smaller versions of lakes. The smallest may be but a few yards across. Our discussion of ponds will be arbitrarily limited to a maximum size of forty acres. These miniature waters dot the landscape in all corners of the United States.

Their mostly fertile waters are the bailiwick of the bluegill angler. Constructed for a variety of purposes such as watershed protection, livestock watering, and recreation, these mostly private jewels provide a nearly unlimited resource for the fly-fisher.

Ponds, particularly those in agricultural regions, tend to age much faster than lakes. There are several possible reasons, the most common being that they fill with eroded sediment from plowed fields, livestock grazing lands, or both. This situation is both good and bad from the fly-fisher's perspective.

On one hand, fertilizer runoff from both sources creates an extremely nutrient-rich environment which produces abundant aquatic vegetation. This makes big bluegills a realistic possibility. The dark side of the issue, however, is that siltation makes the life expectancy of such a pond comparatively short. Grass and tree plantings around the pond's perimeter to help filter runoff will slow the aging process. But while these efforts will help the situation, they cannot change the dynamics of the watershed system. Our search for great bluegill ponds again focuses on the oldest among them. Ponds which are heavily silted have had their sharpest underwater features erased, or at least softened by squishy mud.

The result is good for long-rodders because, in that stage of pond life, most of the fish-holding elements are visible. What you see is what you fish—the moss bed, the weedline, the dam, the spillway, the riprap, the inlet creek, the stump patch, and downed timber. The water, no longer clear and picturesque, may instead invite comparison to a cup of tea. The bluegills don't mind, and a quality fishery may be the result.

Our most dramatic example of the progressive nature of pond aging occurred in our youth. A deep, two-acre pond was created in a heavily wooded area nearly half a mile from the nearest road. Despite the wild setting, the pond drained large fields which were alternately planted in corn and soybeans. The pond was carefully stocked and, because of its remoteness, was rarely fished. This little woodland gem rapidly gained respect as a largemouth bass lunker factory. The bluegills were more sparse, but comparably large.

One night during a heavy downpour, with its spillway blocked by beaver cuttings, the top half of the earthen dam broke. It was never repaired and the once-deep pond was suddenly shallow, reduced to half its original size. Nutrient-rich runoff quickly choked the pond with a tangle of weeds and thick moss beds.

Within one season, the fishery changed dramatically. Small bluegills used the heavy vegetation to take refuge from the big bass and fed heavily on the insect and other small life forms attracted to the weeds. The bass, on the other hand, had a difficult time finding a meal. They had to expend excessive amounts of energy finding food, and the healthy bass population was soon replaced by fish with large heads and skinny bodies.

The bluegill, however, prospered for a short time and grew to gigantic proportions. Each season, the pond became more shallow and more weed-infested. In just a few seasons, there were hardly any pockets left to fish and only poppers or dry flies were possible. Six short but very productive seasons after the dam broke, the pond experienced a complete winterkill. Its life as a pond was over. It existed for another five years as a frog-producing swamp before the once thickly timbered hillsides were cut and the former pond site was incorporated into the adjoining fields of corn and beans. We had witnessed the entire life cycle of a pond at a greatly accelerated pace. It had taken little more than a decade.

Marshes and Swamps

Although dictionaries indicate the terms "marsh" and "swamp" may be used interchangeably, we must make a distinction between the two as fishing environments. Marshes may be described as inundated lowlands heavily overgrown with aquatic plants but having few trees. Swamps, on the other hand, are inundated lowlands heavily overgrown with aquatic plants but having lots of trees.

In marshes, bluegills will use grassy areas with firm bottoms during the spawn. During the summer, fish will seek cooler, shadier water in areas with abundant lily pads or cattails. Access to prime fishing areas in marshes is often greatly hampered by soft mud and tall plants.

Tree roots and deadfalls accompanied by vegetation and zillions of insects make fly-rodding in swamps very productive, but the profusion of trees with low branches that inhibit most casts make fishing here frustrating. Roll casts and short, accurate casts are the keys to success.

Bayous

Bayous are slow-moving, southern tributary streams that connect one body of water with another. They are typically shallow (often no more than eight feet deep) and their width varies from several feet to several yards. They are rich in vegetation and most provide an excellent environment for bluegills. Spawning beds in bayous occupy remarkably large areas and may be continuous for as long as a city block. To find them, look for a firm bottom at the edge of the grass or at the edge of grass near wood structure. Although bayou bluegills seldom stray far from their spawning areas, tree roots may become productive fishing areas in the summer. During mild winters in the South, shallow bluegill fishing can last year round.

Moving Water

Something is stirred in the soul of those who are smitten by moving water. It has a rhythm transcending any combination of poetry and musical style man has ever devised. It is a cleansing experience. This is well understood by our trout- and salmon-seeking brethren but, sadly, not often experienced by bluegill fly-fishers. To accentuate our pleasure, to fully understand our species and, perhaps in the process, to understand ourselves as well, we encourage you to complete the bluegill experience by seeking them in moving water.

In the early 1980s, we spent considerable time camped beside a small stream rarely wider than fifteen feet. The surrounding flora and fauna were both beautiful and abundant, but the major source of our joy was the stream's resident bluegill population. They weren't nearly as large as most pond fish, but they were strikingly beautiful, and had a sense of wildness about them that their stillwater counterparts couldn't match.

We never saw another fisherman on the little stream, and only rarely encountered a hiker or horseback rider along the path that meandered beside its course. More than once we were greeted with a look of curiosity and asked, "Are there trout in here?" Our replies to the contrary always prompted a wry smile and look intended to convey that our sanity was being doubted.

But if trout-fishers sometimes poke into brushy, little-known streams in solitude and return with memories of wild and brightly colored brook trout, are they chastised that their quarry was but four or five inches long? Of course not. They are admired and respected among the brotherhood of fly-fishers for pursuing their beautiful fish in a lovely setting. So, too, should we be.

To understand how to locate bluegills in moving waters, it's only necessary to comprehend the most basic dynamics of the species. Bluegills are creatures of weedy stillwaters. They will not locate in the stream's flow. No game fish, in fact, spends much time in fast water. Instead, they seek something that breaks the current's flow and creates a pocket of much slower water. Any object projecting into the current will create slack water immediately downstream from it. Rocks, log jams, rootwads, overhanging brush, even the intersection of two currents of different speeds will function as a current break.

Trout require only small pockets of slack water. Smallmouth bass and walleye, among others, need little more. Bluegills, on the other hand, seek large areas of currentless water. In essence, then, we are looking for areas of slower-moving streams that have all the characteristics of a lake or pond. Still water and cover will attract and hold the entire bluegill population of the river. Knowing this enables us to focus our attention on a small percentage of the stream.

CHOOSING THE RIGHT WATER

Bluegills that occupy these areas still have a difficult life avoiding predators and coping with the current, especially during periods of high water. The fish, consequently, tend to be smaller in moving water. Whenever we fish this environment, it should be understood that we are sacrificing size to fish here. The beauty and solitude of these waters usually overcomes our natural tendency to seek large fish, but prospecting here also has another side benefit. These bluegills are opportunistic feeders and not usually as selective as their stillwater cousins. They will attack virtually any food source of suitable size. Sizes 12 and smaller flies are usually best suited for this work. Pattern and color are far less a consideration in moving water. Many of these constantly flushed environments simply produce far less bluegill food, thereby causing the fish to be constantly in search of it.

Coal Strip-mine Pits

Easily the most diverse waters are found in coal strip-mine pits. Some provide exceptional fishing, while others are utterly devoid of life. Many are bounded by steep-sided cliffs that plunge into crystal-clear water transformed in its depths to a rich blue reminiscent of an October sky. Don't expect bluegills there. Chances are that gorgeous water is barren, with an unsuitable pH to support any fish.

Certainly pH is as important in lakes and streams as it is in reclaimed strip pits. But while some lake areas are more or less suitable than others, pH in the pits is critical. If a strip-pit trip is in your future, or if there are several pits in your region, it is good advice to separate the good from the bad with a simple pH test. Waters with pH readings much below 5.5 may not support a productive fishery.

Phosphate Strip-pits

Phosphate strip-pits, the result of mining phosphate from resident limestone, are common in Florida and present an unusual fishing situation for both fish and angler. Many are virtually inaccessible due to their high, vertical walls. Vegetation in these "teacups" is limited to plant species that tolerate a very alkaline environment, but little typical bluegill structure is present. Dead or fallen trees, vegetation, rockslides, and the walls themselves may hold some outstanding bluegills.

Good bluegill water has diverse cover such as grass, emergent vegetation, and submerged timber.

Canals

Thousands of miles of water conservation and drainage canals can be found in the low, fertile areas of the Midwest and South. Their composition and contents can vary widely. Some canals are excessively turbid from frequent pumping, and oxygen depletion can be a problem for the fish. While some canals are deep and steep-sided, the most productive canals have low banks and heavy vegetation. Casting to emergent vegetation and trolling the edges can be equally productive. Fish the downwind sides where wind and wave action continually replenish food and oxygen. The entrances of dead-end canals are often filled with debris but there may be an area of clearer water near the trash-filled mouth that will offer good fishing.

Home Waters

Truly versatile bluegill fly-fishers will want to experience success in all of these different environments. By fishing each, and being able to locate and catch numbers of good fish in natural lakes, large impoundments, ponds, and streams, we acquire increased confidence which, in turn, accentuates our skills as bluegill fishermen.

Versatility notwithstanding, however, none of us are ever quite so proficient, nor is our experience quite so pleasurable, as when we are fishing our home water. There we become intimately acquainted with both the fish population and structural elements of the water. We can nearly feel when the fish are ready, and seem to know instinctively what they want and how they want it presented.

For the novice unacquainted with this feeling, it is especially good advice to focus attention on one body of water that can be fished regularly. In the case of large lakes, the emphasis should be on a section of water rather than the whole of it. After fishing it in this manner through all the seasons of a calendar year in different types of weather and conditions, your knowledge will multiply. Then, and only then, will a new bluegill enthusiast feel comfortable enough to be consistently successful in other situations.

The information in this chapter enables us to choose the premier areas of each lake or stream and eliminate the rest. In most situations, ninety percent of the water is unproductive. Armed simply with this knowledge and by fishing only the remaining ten percent, our success will rise dramatically.

Chapter 6
THE BLUEGILL'S SPRING

"SPRING IS SYNONYMOUS WITH FLY FISHING FOR BLUEGILL."

Deke Meyer
Float Tube Fly Fishing
©1989, Frank Amato Publications
Portland, Oregon

The Bluegill's Spring

Just knowing the places bluegills occupy isn't enough. We must be able to predict within narrow limits where the largest concentration of big fish will be located at any given time. To do this, we must understand seasonal and daily changes.

Fishing is often viewed as a sport for early risers or as a late-evening pursuit, but in the early spring we should allow time for the warmth of the day to caress the shallows. That is when we have access to the most active fish.

The bluegill's world is governed by water temperature so a calendar date when spring begins can't be specified, as it can for man. Nor does spring arrive on the same date in all locations. Indeed, southern practitioners of the fly-fishing art may well be fishing summer conditions while northern anglers are still awaiting ice out. But it is reasonable to make some general observations about seasonal fish activity based on water temperatures.

If the water temperature is seventy degrees, whether we're talking about Lake Okeechobee, Florida or Pelican Lake, Minnesota, the bluegills will be involved in the spawning process. Much like their human counterparts, not all bluegills respond to the same stimuli, in the same way, at the same time. While some may get an early start, others will begin to spawn when the temperature gauge says they should be in summer attitude. Bluegills nest several times per year, so there is always a considerable overlap of activities. Our objective is to discover what most of the bigger fish will be doing at a given time, thereby enabling us to maximize our chances of catching more and larger bluegills.

The Pre-spawn Period

In the spring season, the primary interest of sexually mature bluegills is procreation, and movement from their winter depths toward shallower areas begins when the water temperature is about sixty degrees. If you are fortunate enough to fish waters that never fall below that temperature, spawning movement will occur as the water first begins to warm significantly. This doesn't mean that the fish will be in the shallows, only that they will be moving slowly in that direction in a more lascivious frame of mind. Higher water temperature increases their metabolism and, consequently, their need for food. The bluegills will still be located in the deep portions of the emerging weed line. Local weather conditions won't be a strong factor in the fish's behavior at this time because their powerful urge to spawn is dominant. Even intense sunlight penetration into their lairs won't have the negative effect it would have in other seasons. Only a lengthy cold period that significantly drops the water temperature will cause them to retreat into deeper water.

This is also the period when some of the largest bluegills of the season are most vulnerable. They are instinctively driven at this time and, therefore, are much less wary. In addition, their food needs are dramatically increased.

Fly-fishers can capitalize on the bluegill's increasingly active appetite during this early pre-spawn period by using sink-tip line, short leaders, and weighted flies. Cast over deep weed lines and use a "count down" to determine the depth of your fly. By counting, "one-thousand-one, one-thousand-two," etc., you can quickly determine through trial and error where the structure is and at what depth the feeding bluegills are located. It is important to remember that bluegills usually approach our flies with caution, so anything that sinks fast will usually be unattractive to them.

Very light and reflective colors are most productive during this early season. White, and white in combination with silver, get the starting assignment. Because the fish haven't become really active yet, use relatively small hooks. A white marabou streamer with a silver Krystal Flash body, a white rabbit-fur pattern without the tail, a small white-winged streamer, or a white wet pattern will do well. A white Bully's Bluegill Spider is a good choice for this fishing because it sinks at the right rate, yet still has the desired action.

The Spawn

Although the actual distance the bluegills must travel to reach the shallow spawning areas isn't far, the migration may take quite a long time. They will remain in an area awaiting the right conditions to move further. As water temperatures move into the mid-sixties, brightly colored males move onto the shallow flats to build nests, using sweeping motions of their tails to fan away debris. The areas are defended vigorously by nesting males who then attempt to herd or guide nearby ripened females onto the nests. This may occur in water less than six inches deep and has been observed by Lou Vogele in Bull Shoals Lake, Arkansas, in colonies as deep as eight feet.

Small non-nesting males called "sneakers" intrude and release milt when the nesting male is distracted, according to Missouri fisheries biologist Mike Kruse, "The reason they do this is that, if you are a sexually mature four-inch fish, there's just no way you can compete with an eight-inch bluegill, you become a 'sneaker.' Sneakers occupy the area adjacent to the nest in weedy cover. Other small males called 'satellites,' hover around the nest and fertilize eggs by entering the nest as female mimics. When the female comes onto the nest, the 'sneaker' darts in to fertilize her eggs and pass along his genes."

Members of the colony continue to actively spawn for several hours before the females depart for deeper water and leave the nesting males to guard the eggs and fry. "Bluegill, unlike largemouth bass," says Kruse, "do not guard the newly emerged fry very long at all. They guard the eggs, then the fry for only a couple of days after that." When the fry scatter, the males leave for deeper water to feed. In approximately ten days, the process may be repeated. Usually there are four to five breeding periods throughout the spring and summer, but there has been at least one documented observation of the same colony of bluegills spawning nine times in the Mid-south. It's probable that some individual fish spawn even more times during the year in the deep South. It is important to note, however, that after the first spawn, the others occur with diminishing intensity.

Mike Kruse manages his own one-and-a-half-acre pond in central Missouri. "The pond behind my house is heavily infested with water primrose. Every couple of years, I have to vigorously rake the bottom near shore to control it. A couple of years ago in August, I did my raking and when I returned the next day the bottom had been heavily pock-marked by nesting male bluegill."

Many factors, including sunlight penetration, suitable bottom composition, access to deeper water for safe retreats, and the abundance of competing species determine the exact spawning location. The spawning colony may include only a few scattered nests or a vast network closely located to one another which covers the bottom of an entire shallow bay or shoreline. They often appear as light-colored patches against darker surroundings. Even if nests are not easily visible, a few random casts to a shallow area will quickly determine its productivity. Move quickly from place to place until fish contact is made. Once discovered, conditions including depth, bottom composition, and relation to cover should be noted because other similar areas will probably have nesting colonies too. It is also important to remember these areas from year to year because bluegills return to the same place to spawn as long as favorable conditions exist.

When the males are protecting the nests, bluegills (especially large ones) are easy prey for even novice anglers. Virtually any cast that hits the water near these often vast colonies of nest-building males will produce a lusty attack. We should realize, however, that

Pond wading can provide wonderful action,
but take care not to disturb large areas of the silted bottom.

an experienced fisherman with a stealthy approach, gentle presentation, and few misses will catch many more fish during this easiest time of the year.

Use care when approaching bluegill nesting areas. If you are walking the bank, remember that noise will be transmitted to the fish and, since they are probably more shallow than normal, they will be more aware of disturbances.

Boaters should make an equally quiet approach using either a trolling motor, paddle, or pole. It is important not to drift over nesting fish. Anchor off to the side and work the edges before casting to the colony's center. This will prevent a splashy cast or a missed fish from spooking those in the entire area. Then work progressively into the nests as the opportunity dictates. You'll catch many more fish.

It's also important not to disturb the bottom. Motoring, poling, or even paddling disturbs the silt, and can send many bluegills to deeper water. For the same reason, wading and float tubing should only be done if you know the area very well and can approach the beds without disturbing them.

Mike Kruse spent four and a half seasons conducting a bluegill tagging program and his personal observations reinforce those scientific studies. "The largest males are in the center of the colony. They are the most aggressive and, as my tagging study indicates, they are the most likely to be caught."

While the males are preparing and guarding the nests, their primary motivation is to get offensive material (your fly) out the their territory. If you can locate a clearly visible nest with a guarding male, you can demonstrate his protective instinct by dropping a weighted fly with its hook point removed into the nest. He will pick up the fly, carry it outside the nest and drop it. He's not trying to feed, just do his housekeeping. Your choice of fly pattern during the nesting period then isn't critical, and color selection is less important, also.

These brightly colored males are usually aggressive at this time and they often attack much larger fish such as largemouth bass to preserve their efforts. If the nest is located in shallow water, they will usually hit a surface fly as enthusiastically as a wet creation. Small cork or foam poppers are lots of fun at this time. A light-colored bug is a good choice because it is highly visible to the fisherman. Yellow and chartreuse are our personal choices. Sizes 10 and 12 poppers are recommended for midwestern and northern anglers because too many surface strikes are missed when larger hooks are used. Some Southerners prefer their poppers in sizes 6 and 8, but popper manufacturer Tony Accardo is quick to point out that, "even in the South, a larger fly will not necessarily catch bigger fish."

Cast these bugs directly over the spawning beds and let them sit still for a few seconds before making them quiver. If this doesn't elicit a strike, pop them gently until the right retrieve is discovered. It's best to let the fish tell you what and how they want to hit.

Sometimes a louder "pop" is required. It may be irritating to them, or simply necessary to get their attention. When the line and fly are picked up to re-cast, be certain to lift them quietly from the water. If the pickup is snapped, the popper will "ker-plunk" loudly and scare the scales off the fish for several yards in all directions.

Another choice for the shallow spawn is Jack Ellis's Fathead Diver (see page 47). Bluegills may see the Fathead as a tiny frog or miniature injured minnow, but, again, anything that enters their territory is fair game at this time.

Virtually any wet pattern tied on a size 6 to 12 hook will be effective for males on the beds, but anglers may select larger bluegills by using sizes 6 to 8.

If the spawning colony is in shallow water (three feet or less), wet flies with little added weight for slow descent are effective. Suggested patterns are unweighted Woolly Worms and Woolly Buggers, unweighted Bullys, Humbugs, Tellico Nymphs, unweighted Black Gnats, Orange Fish Hawks, and soft-hackle flies.

While color choice isn't critical during the spawn, we may try to match fly color with light-penetration conditions. The brighter the sunlight, the lighter the color we use. The darker the day, the darker the fly. On bright days, the light colors reflect more light and are more visible. Darker days and darker water seem to cause light colors to fade, but a dark pattern enables the fish to see a strong, bold silhouette. Possibly, it is not a particular color that triggers bluegills, but simply their ability to see it most clearly that is important. It is not certain how bluegills perceive color but we believe that some colors are more visible under certain light conditions than others.

Because of past success, many anglers fall in love with a particular color and don't experiment enough to fish other colors with confidence. These fishermen miss a lot of good fishing, as do those who use only one retrieve. Conditions change, and we must change with them or we will only be able to catch fish some of the time, a situation we find most unacceptable.

During the spawn, bluegills will sometimes inhale the fly just as it hits the water. This is very much out of character for them and indicates their hyperactivity. Usually, bluegills approach a fly from the rear, hesitate to evaluate the offering, and then attack it. But now, they hit the fly without reservation.

After the fly splashes down, allow it to rest motionless or fall without action. That alone may provoke a strike. If not, we abandon the usually productive hand-twist retrieve and employ a short strip of two inches to make the fly dart forward before pausing again. Rarely is a long strip on the line a productive retrieve, but during this unique period the bluegills occasionally may see the fly as escaping prey and their aggressive mood could cause them to chase it.

To ensure a positive hook-set, it is important to drop the rod tip to the water, remove slack line, and point the rod tip directly at the fly.

Even huge bluegills have small mouths. Make fly size selection with this in mind.

Only the largest bluegills need to be put "on the reel." Continuing to strip the line and pinning it against the rod handle with your forefinger will usually suffice.

Barbless hooks are best because they enable us to release more fish in better condition. Leave the fish in the water and simply back the hook out. That way your hands won't remove the protective slime that covers the fish's body.

We are not only concerned with protecting fish during the release. We also want to prevent them from racing back through others we intend to catch thus alerting them to be cautious. Where possible, we place the fish in moss or weed beds away from the others. After being caught, they want to hide their faces and pout. Let them. We feel bluegills are a little like Br'er Rabbit—they want the security of a briar patch. If no cover like that exists, at least release the fish on the other side of the boat to prevent them from alarming the others. This is critical to fishing success.

We believe that a hooked fish allowed to fight among the others actually excites them further and makes their capture easier. How many times have you hooked a bluegill and while playing it had another or even several other fish actually peck at the fly stuck in its mouth? This happens so regularly we have concluded that they believe the hooked fish has something of interest and is quickly swimming away to keep them from getting it.

If we capitalize on this competitive urge, it enables us to catch more fish. If you're fishing with a friend, have him cast immediately behind the fish you are fighting. Often, it is possible to tandem-fish like this successfully for long periods as the fish grow increasingly excited.

While the male bluegills are busy building and maintaining the nest and defending their territory, the females wait in nearby deeper water to be escorted to the spawning area. They won't have time to feed, nor do they have any interest in feeding, while they spawn and recover so they are easily tempted to feed now. Although it is difficult to ignore the aggressive males, it is rewarding to discover and catch the heavier females. They will be located nearby, usually at the first breakline in deeper water.

Deep is a relative term, of course, but can mean water from three to eight feet deeper than the corresponding spawning grounds. Females are much more plainly colored, and their undersides are distended with eggs. They are not in a chasing mood at this time, but will readily hit a gently falling or slowly retrieved fly.

Bully flies are a good choice, and we prefer olive or brown colors for this fishing. Woolly Buggers and nymph patterns in natural colors, slowly retrieved, are good, also. For best results, use a sink-tip line or attach a twist-on weight and count the fly down to the fish-holding depth. Release these egg-carrying females with care as they hold the future of our sport.

Actual spawning begins when water temperatures reach sixty-eight to seventy degrees. Neither the male nor female is feeding during this process, yet, as anglers, we sometimes don't notice much of a slowdown in our fishing because others in the colony are still very much in a prespawn attitude and remain catchable. At other times, however, spawning is taking place at such a heated pace that a slowdown is noticeable. Since this can happen within the same fishing trip, it seems very strange to find circumstances so dramatically different when conditions are the same.

To maintain a high level of success we have two choices. We can try a different location on the same body of water or we can move to another body of water where conditions are different. If, for example, we were at first fishing a small pond that warms quickly to the sun's touch, we may be able to find a larger lake that requires considerably more sun and wave action to reach the right temperature. This clearly demonstrates the importance of just a couple of degrees in water temperature and the necessity of carrying and using a thermometer. During the spawn, knowing the temperature can make the difference between understanding where the fish are and what they are doing, or fishing blindly.

The End of the Spawn

When the eggs are deposited and fertilized, the female retreats slowly to deeper water. She will remain deep and in a negative feeding attitude for a short time as she recovers. The male, on the other hand, will occupy a battle station near the nest to protect it from predation. The incubation process takes from two to five days depending on conditions, and the males remain to protect their brood of fry. They may play protective parent for a couple of days, allowing the fry to acclimate themselves. When this instinct has worn thin, however, they turn on their offspring, inhaling several as the young scatter to find cover and begin fending for themselves. Any light-colored pattern fished with a quick darting motion may attract the attention of these cannibalistic males.

Spring is the season that persuades many that bluegills are too easy for advanced anglers and therefore suitable only for beginners and children. Disdainful anglers apparently have an aversion to catching a hundred fish or more in an evening. We do not. If it is wary and selective fish they want, these same bluegills will offer them the ultimate challenge in the summer season.

Chapter 7
THE BLUEGILL'S SUMMER

"SELECTIVE BREAM? YES, INDEED."

Gary Borger
The Sunfishes
©1993, Abenaki Publishers, Inc.
Bennington, Vermont

The Bluegill's Summer

Summer is a season of abundance. Aquatic insects, both nymphal and adult, are plentiful. The other spawning species have produced a smorgasbord of fry, and larger bluegills feed heavily on them. For bluegills, life takes on a more leisurely pace.

Although spawning may continue throughout the summer, it proceeds with diminishing intensity. Casting to the same places that were successful during the spring spawn reveals fewer fish using the shallow spawning beds. Fisheries biologists say that electro-fishing and trap-setting are less productive in the summer than during spring, indicating that many fish have moved out of the shallows.

Where have they gone?

Most move to deeper holding areas, then onto the shallow flats to feed during periods of low light. The deeper location prevents bright sunlight from restricting their vision, and offers more comfortable water temperatures. If the shallows are heavily covered with moss or weeds, bluegills may remain there where they are protected and cooled by the dense vegetation. They may also remain shallow for long periods if there is heavy cloud cover. Young, small bluegills are likely to remain in shallow water throughout the summer because they are dependent on the resident vegetation for food and protection. They are at great risk in the open depths prowled by large predators.

Precisely how deep large bluegills locate depends on many factors. Sunlight penetration, water temperature, food availability, protective cover, oxygen levels, and pH balance are among the most significant. We need to be constantly aware of three of these factors.

Adult bluegills will rarely be without protective cover, an available food source, and a comfortable water temperature. If all three are suitable for the fish and hookups remain elusive, the other factors should be examined to see what caused the lack of success.

The depth at which bluegills spend midday is also determined by the characteristics of the water. In very deep, clear lakes with little or no vegetation, bluegills may locate at twenty or thirty feet, while in a shallow, murky lake, the holding depth might be only four or five feet. Generally, older and more fertile lakes have more shallow-holding bluegill populations and, consequently, the angler has greater access to them.

Deep-water Adjustments

Where summer bluegills tend to reside in ten or more feet of water, sink-tip lines, added fast-sinking sections, and heavily weighted flies are standard for midday fishing. Movements into the shallows to feed usually occur early in the morning and late in the evening. As summer advances, fish spend progressively less time there.

Use of a fish locator is helpful unless the water is very familiar and good bluegills have been caught in the same locations before. Once the population is found, triangulating the location and keeping careful notes helps ensure that we can return to productive spots easily.

Triangulation is accomplished by finding three permanent objects on shore, all in different directions, then visualizing the intersecting lines from these points so that they meet at your location. By marking the locations in a notebook, you can return to the spot on subsequent trips.

In large impoundments, these locations may be a considerable distance from shore. A long point which extends gradually into the water or a submerged island in mid-lake are two obvious examples. Like the spawning grounds in spring, these summer locations will be productive year after year.

Once the fish have been located and you've selected the correct line and fly to get down to them, cast well beyond the fish. Line does not sink straight to the bottom. Rather, it sinks in an arc bowing toward you. Without an extra-long cast, your fly may miss the fish entirely.

Each time you strip the line to impart action, pause to let the fly sink back into the fish zone. The deeper the fly when it's hit by a fish, the quicker and harder we must set the hook. Longer distance and water pressure cause the line to be misaligned with the rod tip. Consequently, the rod tip must be moved farther to remove slack and overcome the stretch of the line. In this situation, we've used seven-weight rods to facilitate hook-setting on exceptionally deep fish.

Fly Selection, Some Considerations

For deep-holding fish, we use heavily weighted patterns such as the Cajun Coachman, Yuk Bugs, and micro-jigs. We also use streamers and darker colors of our Bully's Bluegill Spider pattern.

Streamers are a good summer choice because minnows and fry are abundant at this time. We tie them on size 10, 2XL hooks and use wing materials that don't extend much beyond the hook bend so that short strikes will not be missed. We use a perfect-bend hook with a turned-down eye, but a Limerick bend makes some sense because of the smaller gap.

In very fertile older lakes with murky water and dense vegetation, we expect to find bluegills fairly shallow in the daytime. These fish must be approached differently from their clear-water cousins. There may be a problem getting the fly through the salad bowl that the fish are using to avoid sunlight and cool themselves. We've seen some really dense situations that could only be fished with weedless surface bugs. Under most circumstances, we regard monofilament weed guards as "fishless" because they prevent good hook-sets, but in these extremely frustrating situations they may be the only option. Make the best of it by sharpening your hooks and setting them with increased gusto.

Casting accuracy will be at a premium. Floating moss or very thick vegetation leave the caster only small pockets in which to land and manipulate a bug. We prefer a dark-colored popper body that includes alternating bands of black and yellow because bees and wasps are a preferred food and also because the yellow band is more visible to us on the water's dark, intricately patterned background. Sizes 10 and 12 have favored status in our fly boxes. In situations which allow more room to work the fly, small fathead divers are an excellent choice.

Choosing Naturals

Volumes have been written (primarily by trout enthusiasts) about "matching the hatch," and creative fly tiers spend countless hours replicating stoneflies, caddisflies, and mayflies. Of these, only mayflies play a role in the stillwater bluegill's life.

Nevertheless, it is helpful to understand the importance of insects in the bluegill's environment. Here, mosquitoes, craneflies, midges, dragonflies, damselflies, and numerous terrestrial insects including grasshoppers, crickets, ants, bees, and moths, become important.

One very special example of a specific insect hatch's importance occurs each May in Lake Okeechobee, Florida, and in similar waters nearby. A species of blind mosquito, called "chizzy-wink," emerges by the millions. In the words of native fly-fishing author, Jon Cave, "The bream just go crazy." Chizzy-winks can be matched by the mosquito pattern given on page 46, but don't be concerned with matching fly size to the actual insect. In this situation, bluegills will take oversized patterns as readily as tiny reproductions.

While matching insects will sometimes increase success, most of the time only small bluegills are caught during a hatch. At first, we thought these aggressive little fish were simply beating the big ones to our flies but, through experimentation, we were eventually convinced that this was only the upper layer of aquatic-feeding activity.

Beauty, tenacity, availability, and selectivity make bluegill the perfect fly rod species.

As the small fish population feeds on the hatch, large bluegills move into the deeper layer below to feed on nymphs or small minnows. Very often, observing a hatch or lots of feeding minnows alerts us to fish a small streamer below the primary layer of activity. Large bluegills are voracious minnow feeders. We tend to associate this foraging activity with largemouth bass because we have often seen bass charge recklessly through insect-feeding baitfish sending them spraying in all directions. Large bluegills, however, are more subtle and much more challenging to catch than bass. They grab the minnows that attempt to flee toward the bottom and capitalize on those injured in the fracas.

Selectivity

Large bluegills are cautious opportunists that often reject any fly not presented in a lifelike manner. In our pre-catch-and-release days, we cleaned and examined the stomach contents of lots of fish, including trout, bass, crappie and, of course, bluegills. All of the others frequently swallowed some debris such as small pieces of sticks, pebbles, or snail casings, but bluegills did not.

Largemouth bass are ambush predators so the presence of debris is easy to understand, but trout are known for their selectivity. This evidence, and observations of feeding fish, persuade us that bluegills are among the most selective of all freshwater fish.

Fishing for "Cruisers"

One of the most unusual bluegill-fishing situations occurs on some summer ponds and lakes after the water has warmed and Chironomid larvae or midge hatches rise into the surface film. Bluegills form tightly woven schools which cruise irregularly around the surface of the pond. Even in murky water, this activity is quite visible as the dorsal fins and backs of the fish are often out of the water. These schools of "cruisers" are comprised of fish of the same year class and therefore are of the same size. They have abandoned the protection of their cover and are very wary.

This is an excellent opportunity to use dry flies and emergers. We carry some size 16 and 18 dry flies, including Black Gnats and Renegades, just for this fishing situation. Cast to the side or in front of the school, but never to the middle of it. Identify the lead fish and always approach the school from the side. Casting over them, allowing your shadow to fall on them, or missing a strike will likely put them down. Often these roving packs of panfish are small, but try dropping a weighted nymph behind them. Larger fish will often feed opportunistically on swimming nymphs.

The trick is hooking one of these fish at the edge of the school and playing it away from the rest. This won't spook the school, but it's quite opposite our normal approach when fighting bluegills among their brethren to create the illusion of a feeding binge.

It can be very difficult to keep up with the rapidly advancing school without spooking it, but float tubes are ideal for this task. Cruisers tend to change direction abruptly, so despite their lack of speed, maneuverability and stealth make float tubes superior to ordinary watercraft in this fishing situation.

Fishing a Hatch

Dry flies have another application for the summer bluegill hunter. Early mornings and late evenings will bring forth abundant insect hatches which trigger feeding activity. Here, we are less concerned with small dries and usually a nicely visible attractor pattern in size 10 or 12 will do the job.

We subscribe to the theory, "the bigger the fly, the bigger the fish," but we keep in mind that even the world's record bluegill, at 4 pounds 12 ounces, still has a very small mouth. So, while the theory is applicable to largemouth bass, we can also apply the principle to bluegills by utilizing relatively larger flies.

Bluegills don't need to chase their food during summer's abundance and are normally disinclined to move either far or fast to intercept our flies. A very slow retrieve is usually most productive. Big-bluegill specialist, Walt Holman, a northern Alabama native, advises, "My best summertime retrieve is to do nothing, then do just a little bit, with long pauses in between." It's good advice.

The "Dog Days"

In late summer, the so-called "dog days," even big bluegills tend to favor smaller food forms. Again, size is relative. If your size-10 patterns were successful earlier and, as the summer progresses, those offerings are being ignored more frequently, try switching to size 12 of the same pattern. Matching the hatch is both productive and satisfying, but most of the time it is unnecessary.

Attractor patterns such as the Professor and Grizzly King may remain effective throughout the entire summer season. We believe size adjustment and color selection are more important than accurately replicating aquatic or terrestrial insects. This statement, however, requires qualification, because it is not true all of the time. Why game fish will suddenly abandon one predictable feeding pattern, even when the food form appears to be abundant, then select something else remains a mystery. It's just one of those delicious little puzzles that makes our sport so fascinating.

Low-light conditions are not only favorable for traditional dry-fly patterns. Many bluegill enthusiasts carry nothing but little poppers for these early morning and late-evening excursions and do well most of the time. A closed-cell sponge spider with wiggly rubber legs can skim along almost silently and provoke dramatic attacks, too. We are particularly fond of sponge spiders in yellow because they are easily visible to us, but black is more effective on overcast days, early and late in the day, and when fishing dark,

Float tubing ponds during low light conditions allows anglers access to shallow-feeding bluegills.

murky water after a summer shower. Generally, we believe that small, well-fished poppers and spiders will outproduce a matching dry, but we are always prepared for the exception.

Using the Wind

Changing weather conditions can dramatically affect summer bluegills' behavior. One of those conditions, wind, can create feeding opportunities that otherwise would not exist. Fish may interpret a rough surface as safe overhead cover, or they may simply use the wind to bring them food.

In locations where there is a high bank with tall grass or weeds, probe the windward side of the pond or lake with terrestrial patterns. As grasshoppers, ants, beetles, and other insects are blown onto the surface of water, opportunistic bluegills will feed heavily, even at midday.

The best presentation requires a boat or float tube so that casts can be made close to shore while using the wind to help drift the fly over the fish. The opposite shore, where wave action is greatest, will also be productive. Here, the fish are waiting for food to be washed to them, and, again, the best cast from shore or near shore is directly into the teeth of the wind.

If waves are significant enough to create a murky water line, it may become a structural, fish-holding element. Be opportunistic by retrieving your fly right through it or along its edge.

Sunlight

Bright sunlight is the enemy of large bluegills and, consequently, of fishermen. Usually, our quarry will retreat to deeper holding structure and remain there until lower light conditions arrive in the form of cloud cover or lower angles of the sun. Through experience on frequently fished home waters or by using a locator, we can still find and catch bluegills in deep water.

The most difficult situation for us is not the consistently bright, sunny day, but one when the sun frequently plays hide-and-seek among the clouds. Fish eyes adjust to changes in light very slowly. They may need as much as thirty minutes to complete their transition from bright to overcast. It may be that, after several false starts, fish simply become confused and wait to feed until light conditions stabilize. Even when we can locate fish under these conditions, they appear to be in a negative feeding attitude and are difficult to catch.

Dealing With Suspended Fish

Large summer bluegills will also suspend at shallow depths over very deep water. A fish locator may be the only clue to their location. If shallow and usually reliable deep structures are producing poorly, turn on the locator and actively look for suspended fish. Sunlight penetration and warm water temperatures may have driven the bluegills deeper, but active largemouth or some other predator species may have forced them away from deep structure as well. Suspended bluegills occur a lot more frequently in less fertile water because they may simply have run out of options.

Once the fish are located, anchor the boat, cast weighted flies on sink-tip line (full-sinking line if the fish are deeper than eight feet), and count your presentation down to the fish-holding level. With patience, this tactic can be successful. If there is a little breeze, drift over the spot while dragging weighted flies through the fish.

It is usually necessary to substantially extend leaders for this presentation. We've added as much as ten feet of tippet material to get down to the fish. While this kind of fishing demonstrates the versatility of bluegill fly-fishers, it is not, in our opinion, pleasurable fishing.

Three factors account for our decreased enjoyment. First, the rewarding act of casting is subtracted from the experience. Second, strike detection becomes increasingly difficult as the fly's depth increases. As the distance between the strike and rod tip increases, the time required to feel the hit increases, too. In deep water, a fish can easily examine and reject the fly before it's felt by the angler. Finally, achieving a good hook-set becomes more difficult due to line stretch and bowing of the line.

If the fish are particularly deep, fishing in this manner becomes a vertical jigging operation and it can be extremely effective if the fish are active. Use a trolling motor to adjust your drift and to re-position the boat. (More about this in Chapter Nine.)

We have a fishing friend that regularly uses float tubes equipped with locators and he is equally successful with these suspended fish.

Wood Structure

We have a decided preference for wood structure. One of the lakes we regularly fish is almost devoid of emergent vegetation, but is crowded with standing and submerged timber. Very careful boat handling and cautious presentations are essential. If the boat is allowed to drift freely, it might constantly bang into one tree after another, each collision producing a gigantic "thud." In the time it takes to tie on a new fly, we may negatively impact fishing in an entire cove.

Another problem with fishing these submerged forests is presenting flies that don't hang up on every cast. Monofilament weed guards are one choice, but we dislike them and use them only when all else fails. Other choices are keel and bendback flies which ride upside down, thus enabling the hook to slide over most projections, but they are difficult to find in sizes appropriate for bluegills so we create our own by weighting flies with barbell eyes. This also causes the hook to ride upside down and can dramatically reduce unwanted hookups. When tying these self-styled keel flies, bear in mind the pattern must be inverted on the hook as well.

Other highly favored wood structures are boat docks and marinas. These manmade forests provide large, shaded areas and many hiding places, but not all docks are created equal. Some hold great numbers of fish, while others will hold none at all.

The best docks have two characteristics. Most importantly, the dock must have access to deep water nearby. If our prospective dock extends from shallow shoreline into additional shallow water and it's some distance from the nearest drop-off, it won't hold many large fish. If, however, the dock extends from shallow to relatively deep water, it may be a good producer. The other requirement is additional cover. If weeds, moss, or even submerged Christmas trees are present, the dock will hold fish.

Bully's Bluegill Spider, Woolly Buggers, and small streamers are good producers here. Fish the deeper areas along the docks first, then work progressively shallower. This will prevent your casts from spooking other fish nearby. If, however, you have determined that good-sized fish are consistently located at the back or shallow portion of the docks, maximize your efforts by casting only to that area, then fish as many docks as possible. Carefully position your boat so that you can cast to all of the potentially productive areas.

In water where crayfish are abundant, their imitation can be tremendously successful. Most game fish find crayfish irresistible. Large bluegills are no exception, but flies should represent the young soft-shelled version in light, translucent colors. Patterns should not exceed one inch in length, and sizes 8 and 10 are best.

The summer season provides the greatest challenge to the bluegill enthusiast. The larger fish are selective and very sensitive to weather changes, but producing some of these tougher fish can be very rewarding.

Iowa-based tackle representative David Halblom agrees. "Under most circumstances, bluegill are looked at as something for the kids to fish for. I just don't understand that at all. I'm accustomed to catching ten- to twelve-inch bluegill and, especially in the summer period, it is tremendously challenging and exciting sport."

During this season, even veteran anglers can find large bluegill fishing a humbling experience.

Chapter 8
As the Water Cools

"DURING THE MORE THAN FIFTY YEARS I SPENT IN THE MANUFACTURING END OF FISHING TACKLE, I HAD THE GOOD FORTUNE TO CATCH MANY OF THE EXOTIC FISH SPECIES IN MUCH OF THE WORLD. MY FRIENDS ALMOST INVARIABLY STARE IN DISBELIEF WHEN I TELL THEM THAT ONE OF MY FAVORITE FISH IS THE BLUEGILL."

Leon Chandler
©1994, <i>The Flyfisher</i>
Keokee Publishing
Sandpoint, Idaho

As the Water Cools

As water temperatures begin to cool, bluegills spend longer periods of time on the shallow flats. There are several reasons. Cooler water tells them that winter is approaching, and instinctively they prepare for the rigors of the cold season. Of even greater significance, however, is the lower angle of the sun's rays. These two factors encourage the fish to forage the shallows longer. Autumn also is a time when the daylight period becomes shorter. Fish are aware of this change and it's also responsible for the increase in feeding intensity referred to by some as the "fall frenzy."

As autumn progresses, it becomes more and more important to fish the middle of the day so that the sun can warm the thin water. In many ways, this is the most enjoyable season in which to pursue bluegills. Beautiful fall colors, a crispness in the air, shallow and aggressively feeding fish, and long midday trips are ample reasons to extend the fishing season. Autumn can be a time of rapid change best understood by consulting the temperature gauge. Northern anglers will find their waters cool much more rapidly than those in the South. Especially in the north, anglers must be aware of making rapid adjustments in location and presentation which can easily change dramatically from day to day. Because of this, many bluegill fishermen simply hang up their rods for the season or continue to hope to catch hungry bream on the flats just one more time. The bluegills do, in fact, invade the shallows during autumn and can feed frenetically, but often this period is brief. Bluegill fly-fishers can, however, remain consistently successful by understanding what the fish are doing at a specific time during autumn. The progression of the season remains the same, whether north or south.

While each of the seasons can be viewed as a series of separate stages, this is particularly true of autumn. We can use water temperatures as a guide to understand what most of the bluegills are doing as the season advances. By dividing autumn into four separate stages, we can focus on the locations and feeding attitude of the majority of the fish while understanding that, once again, there is considerable overlap in fish behavior.

Post-Summer

We refer to stage one as post-summer because the temperatures have just started to drop. If the water has been in the mid-eighty-degree range, for example, water temperatures will fall rather slowly into the mid-seventies as cooler evenings, shorter days, and decreased sunlight angle begin to take their toll. The days may remain warm, but evenings are cool and water temperatures begin to decline.

Fly Selection

Bluegills make only minor adjustments in their feeding habits at this time. Morning and evening trips into the shallows are now for extended periods of time. Fish may still be quite selective because the abundant food sources of summer are still in place. Natural colors such as olive, brown, and black are good choices, and there are times when terrestrial patterns such as crickets, grasshoppers, and ants fished in the surface film are good choices. Just as in the summer season, continue to fish slowly as bluegills aren't yet in a chasing mode.

In contrast to the late-summer season, larger flies are in order again post-summer. The reason may be twofold. First, the larger meal may seem more attractive in the cooler water, but also this is a time that finds bluegills of all sizes sharing the same flats, and the smaller fish simply must become more aggressive or miss out on vital meals. We use size 8 flies almost exclusively during post-summer, and like to crawl our own Bully flies across the flats. Minnow imitators also remain hot.

This is an enjoyable time to float or wade a slow-moving stream. We nearly always begin these trips with a nymph pattern, but if surface-feeders are noticed, as they often are, a small popper or size 12 dry fly can add some fun. Slow-flowing waters which gently caress a graveled bottom are a good place to begin prospecting post-summer. Nymphs should be drifted naturally with the current and lifted occasionally in the slow water to simulate a hatch. Dries should be fished with a natural drift also, of course, but small poppers are most effective when retrieved with a fast but steady rhythm. While it is always good advice to keep an open mind and let the bream choose the menu and presentation style, this late-summer stream pattern has been consistent enough for us in a variety of waters to recommend for your consideration.

On large impoundments with vast shallow gravel bars and shorelines, post-summer offers a situation that produces consistent catches of big bluegills. Late afternoon sun may induce a hatch of large mayflies. We have rarely observed any surface-feeding activity with this hatch, and dry-fly imitations are ignored. Nearly any dark wet pattern, however, that is allowed to sink to the gravel and is then lifted as an emerger has a chance of being inhaled by big bluegills. Despite the large size of the adult insects, we always do best with size-10 and smaller versions of the North Fork Nymph and Bully's Bluegill Spider. This mayfly hatch has so consistently produced for us that post-summer late afternoons on our favorite graveled lake are spent cruising likely areas until we see the adult insects coming off the water. This pattern lasts well into the second stage of autumn or until water temperatures dip into the mid-sixty-degree range.

Early Autumn

Stage two of the fall season or early autumn will find mid-seventy-degree water temperatures tumbling into the mid-sixties, and this promotes some significant changes. Bluegills seem to understand that the time of abundance is coming to an end. In lakes and ponds, they are on the shallow flats nearly all day now, foraging and chasing when the circumstances permit. Bluegills abandon their penchant for summer selectivity, and anything of appropriate size seems to be fair game. Brighter flies that are highly visible for longer distances are appropriate in early autumn. Chartreuse, silver, and especially hot pink are good choices. Faster retrieves with lots of built-in action become a lethal trigger as the fish apparently are convinced these attractive meals are about to escape.

While bluegills are active and not very selective at this time, they are still quite skittish because the water is clearing and sunlight may illuminate the shallows. In addition, shadows can be a significant problem and wearing clothing that blends into the background can be even more significant in autumn than at other times. Lighter tippets that enable the angler to avoid splashy presentations and a stealthy approach to these shallow but nervous fish, while always in vogue, are essential now.

Fly patterns aren't nearly so critical a choice in early autumn. It is nearly as easy to produce a good number of large bluegills at this time as during the spawn. But mistakes have to be minimized. Eager and aggressive, these hungry fish can disappear from the shallows faster than at any other time.

Stream fishing in early autumn is especially productive. If water temperatures are dropping rapidly, large bluegills will ignore caution and pursue a meal for long periods all over slow pools.

These chasers feed at the surface over relatively deep bottoms. Topwater selections, while effective now, aren't the only viable choice. We also use larger flies now than at any other time in streams, but this choice should be made on the basis of potential fish size.

Middle-Autumn

Fall's third stage, or the middle autumn period, will see water temperatures between 65 and 55 degrees. Bluegills make brief but frenetic forays into the shallowest waters, usually during the warmest period of the day (mid-afternoon). But as this stage progresses, they will spend most of the day on the deepest section of the flats. This may mean water between three and four feet in depth. Their activity remains extremely high, and jolting strikes are common as the bluegill's urgency to enter the winter season in prime condition intensifies.

Again, highly visible colors are called for, but both fly size and speed of the retrieve should be reduced as the water temperature drops. Fluorescent yellow in size 10 becomes our favorite as water temperatures plummet into the upper fifties.

To enjoy the last period of the season's fast fishing, the flyfisher's timing must be right. Fishing the flats is only productive for a brief time each day, and that period shortens as the water cools. If repeated casts to the shallows are unproductive, try moving to the deepest part of the flats. Slow retrieves are best on this deep edge. We use brightly colored patterns with enticing action in both locations, but, while the patterns are similar to the early autumn period, smaller sizes (10 and 12) are best. One notable exception is the use of a heavily-weighted white Woolly Worm tied with a short, red marabou tail (see page 48) and fished slowly along the deep flats.

Middle autumn is an excellent time to use double casts of flies. This tactic is most common in the South, but it is just as effective in northern waters. It not only enables the angler to use two or more flies, but allows him the opportunity to fish different depths, patterns, and types of flies in a single cast.

One technique for assembling a "tandem rig" involves tying on one fly pattern, then, using a thumbnail, simply sliding the knot to the side of the hook eye before attaching a second piece of tippet

"Indian summer" warms the shallows for extended periods during the day.

material to the other side. The length and size of the secondary tippet may be varied to suit the fly chosen as the "dropper." The two lines seldom entangle one another and exciting double hook-ups are reasonably common. Landing two eight- to ten-inch bluegills on a three-weight rod is a thrill for even the most experienced fisherman.

In streams, it is still possible to encounter chasing bluegills but this occurs for increasingly shorter periods of time. At other times, the larger fish will be in the shallows foraging. Well-placed and gentle casts will be productive. Usually the hits are subtle, and you should watch the line carefully for any hesitation. We particularly like to use small wet patterns in sizes 12 and 14 in middle-autumn stream fishing. The Grizzly King and Professor are personal favorites.

Late Autumn

During the final stages of fall, or the late-autumn period, water temperatures will tumble from 55 degrees until freeze-up occurs. The fish abandon the shallows at this time and utilize the first break line or deepest edge of the weedline. This may involve water from four feet to fifteen-plus feet deep.

If your water contains standing timber, bluegills often suspend in the treetops during this period. Bluegills tend to group in late autumn by year class, so locating a population of larger fish is the first objective. It is also possible that several treetops will contain a range of sizes, but the larger fish are usually found in the thickest cover where the branches are most forked. When they are suspended in the treetops, flies with weed guards or flies that ride with the hook-up, keel fly, or bendback style, are usually required.

Bluegills also suspend over deep water away from cover if that is the only pattern available to them during late autumn. Fishing suspended fish in open water has its own set of problems. First, locating the fish in larger water can be difficult. Using a locator is easily the best solution, but trolling or drifting the mouths of coves, along steep bluffs, or off the edges of extended points can also be effective.

Sometimes, staying on these fish is more difficult than locating them. The problem is that it's unusually hard to anchor a boat in water this deep, and if wind is a factor it becomes even more complicated to both stay on the fish and make a good presentation.

The best tactic is to have one angler handle the boat and watch the locator and another to fish. If you are fishing this situation alone, a controlled drift using the trolling motor to maintain the correct path and motoring back through the suspended fish is the best method. This method of drifting with the wind, then slowly trolling back through the fish really involves a vertical jigging type of presentation. The key element is speed control as the fly must be fished very slowly.

Fishing streams in the late-autumn period can help extend the season by a week or more. If a stream is spring-fed, it will remain warmer longer and the movement of the water may help some, too. Rivers normally are running at the season's lowest in terms of water level. This forces bluegills and, indeed, all fish species to use the deepest portions of the remaining holes. Competition for available food in a given hole usually intensifies with time. You can find some remarkably fast fishing in streams in late autumn, even when the other options have slowed dramatically. White or silver is our best color during late autumn and size-12 flies are best for these increasingly lethargic fish.

Winter

For sections of the country where bluegill water freezes over in winter, the fly-fishing season is over. Bluegills can be caught through the ice, certainly, but not with conventional fly-fishing methods. It is time to retire to the tying vise, switch species, or plan a trip to a warmer climate.

If your favorite waters remain open, the bluegills will continue to locate in the late-fall areas, and the same tactics will remain effective. Unfrozen ponds can still be fished effectively throughout winter. Locate the deepest water nearest the summertime feeding flats. Bluegills may suspend, or in shallow ponds locate near the bottom.

If the water temperature is in the 30- or 40-degree range, many of the fish will be in a neutral to negative feeding mood. Persistence is vital to success. If some are hungry, we can begin to slowly pick up the more active fish. In doing so, other fish may become stimulated by the activity and become more aggressive.

The longer the water temperature remains in the 40-degree range, the more bluegills will suspend. In relatively shallow ponds, they may suspend over open water without relating directly to a structural element. They may, for example, be located in four feet over a ten-foot bottom. It is important to count-down your offering and fish it very slowly.

The only way to be certain of the fish's location beforehand is by scouting with a locator. This task is made somewhat easier because they tend to spread out horizontally and are, therefore, scattered over a considerable area. They are also usually grouped by year class, but it's our experience that the biggest fish are located in the center.

It may appear that these larger fish are most easily caught by dropping the fly into the center. That isn't true. If the center can be determined (sometimes that's not as easy as it sounds), we've enjoyed our best success by fishing the outer edges first, then moving progressively into the larger fish. We believe the reason for this is that the feeding fish tend to excite the larger bream thereby putting them in a more positive feeding mood. Again white is our choice of color and small sizes are essential. Speed of the retrieve should be only slightly faster than dead still. On larger lakes with available deep water, this is the time to use heavily weighted flies, full-sinking lines, and seven-weight rods. Vertical jigging techniques allow the angler to maintain the most direct contact possible with the fly. The heavy rod is needed to remove slack quickly in the hook-set and is equally important in steering hooked fish away from the submerged brush or tree limbs these cold-water fish seek out.

Our most consistent success with late-season bluegills in big waters has come using an extra-heavy white marabou micro-jig. Most of our efforts are concentrated in standing timber but we've had some success in deep water at the base of rock bluffs. In each case the best technique is to very slowly raise the rod tip, then very slowly lower it. Don't allow the jig to fall freely, but keep it under control. Repeat this process for several minutes before trying a different location. Even these changes should only be slight adjustments in location. Move slowly and be very patient. An interested fish may have seen your first efforts but in its lethargy wasn't motivated strongly enough to move for it. A small adjustment in location may do the trick.

Those who live near spring-fed streams that have good populations of bream can easily overcome the wintertime slowdown. A sizable spring will attract and hold active fish but they must be approached carefully. Sloppy presentations will put the fish down, and it will be a long walk to the next spring hole. Careful casts using long, fine tippets are a must. North Fork Nymphs dropped quietly into these pools have provided our best action, but Gold Ribbed Hare's Ear Nymphs are a good second choice.

The rewards of the winter bluegill season lie in catching these difficult fish when few others are doing so and, of course, in the joy of fishing in complete solitude.

Chapter 9
EFFECTIVE PRESENTATIONS

"NO MATTER HOW CLEVERLY, CUNNINGLY THESE FLIES ARE TIED, THEY'RE ONLY AS EFFECTIVE AS HOW WELL YOU PLACE AND ANIMATE THEM. YOU ARE THE KEY TO THEIR ULTIMATE EFFECTIVENESS."

Dave Whitlock
L. L. Bean Fly Fishing for Bass Handbook
©1988, L. L. Bean, Inc.

Effective Presentations

Intimate knowledge of bluegill behavior, an equally solid understanding of the bluegill's environment, and knowledge of how bluegill behavior is affected by the change of seasons and weather conditions is not, unfortunately, a guarantee that anglers can catch fish. To be successful, fly-fishers must be able to present their offerings in a manner that causes fish to want to hit the flies. Yet many fishermen believe catching fish depends solely on the delivery of the fly and, therefore, casting prowess solves the entire problem. Despite the importance of casting accuracy, occasionally for long distances, casting proficiency is but a small part of the presentation picture.

Several seasons ago we hosted a fisherman who described himself as a knowledgeable and experienced fly-fisher. He was anxious to experience the large bluegills we had described to him, but unfortunately came to fish during a week-long cold snap in April that had backed the fish off the flats into deeper water. We knew that we'd have to relocate the bluegills and took for granted that as an experienced fly-fisher, he understood that as well.

It was difficult work. The constant wind was cold and blustery. Finally, after spending all morning and part of an afternoon checking several small lakes for wind conditions and water temperatures while we scouted the area by running the locator, we discovered two bunches of fish.

One was suspended off a secondary point in a cove. We back-trolled over them using full-sinking lines, short leaders, and small streamers. The other was holding in brush at the base of a steep ravine. For these we anchored within an easy cast of the fish and used floating line, long leaders, and counted down our weighted flies. Eventually, we caught and released thirty-five hand-sized bluegills.

At dinner our "expert" wondered aloud how many we might have caught had we "gotten started" earlier. The urge to inflict bodily harm has never been stronger.

Presentation must be viewed as consisting both of methods and a delivery system. Presentation methods refer to the angler's approach to the fishing situation. Choices include bank-stalking and any of the numerous methods of placing the fly-fisher either in or on the water. In discussing delivery systems, we address the specific way in which the fly is presented to the fish.

Bank Fishing

First, let us examine the methods of presentation beginning with the simplest, yet most misunderstood form: walking the bank. Those who primarily fish ponds use this method almost exclusively, yet it is performed poorly most of the time with disappointing results.

Bank-bound anglers should pay attention to their selection of clothing and accessories, especially when fishing clear water where there may be fish feeding in the shallows. Tops and pants should blend with the surroundings. No aquatic inhabitant is accustomed to seeing a brightly-colored T-shirt bouncing along its shore. Similarly, highly reflective watches and sunglasses also send a signal of caution into the bluegill's lair.

Perhaps the worst offenses occur during the fisherman's approach. In small environments, sounds are readily transmitted to the fish. Dropping an object on the bank or heavy footsteps send waves of unusual sounds to the bluegills. Immediately the fish are more cautious and the job of catching them has just become unnecessarily more difficult.

Successful bank-bound anglers approach the water very much like hunters. They must be quiet and alert, blend with the surroundings, and learn about the conditions they are about to fish before making their first casts.

After locating the area believed to hold fish, they should search for just the right position from which to cast. The best location will enable fly-casters to cover an entire area from one spot while blending into the background. It is important to keep in mind possible shadows from the angler's body and rod when selecting a potential casting location. Wind direction and velocity are also important considerations. Strong winds interfere with pleasurable casting, while more gentle winds can be utilized to help shield the angler from the fish's view.

An opportunistic angler should note that a stiff breeze also helps wash food to the bluegills. Therefore, one choice casting location may be on the bank facing the wind. By throwing a tight loop directly into the wind, the fly can be drifted naturally toward the fish, who will also be facing the wind waiting for a meal. Diagonal casts are undesirable in this particular location because the wind will blow the line toward the bank. Cover the diagonal areas by stepping down the bank and recasting directly into the wind at each new position.

When fishing ponds where wind is not a factor, fan casting the suspected productive area while probing various depths will quickly tell fly-fishers exactly where the fish are located. Noting the location and depth of the strikes and applying the information to new locations will increase the catch.

Fan Casting

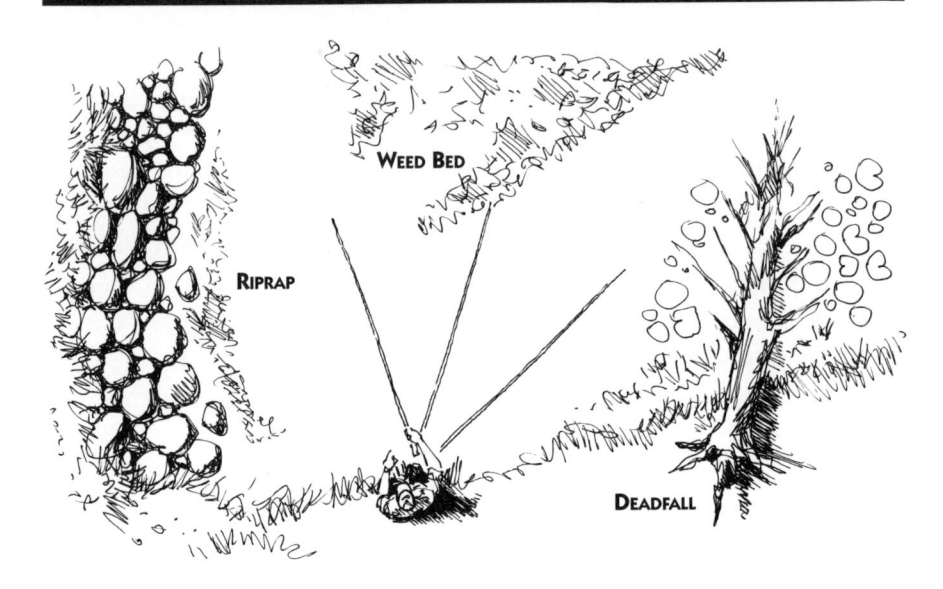

Riprap

Weed Bed

Deadfall

Several different types of structure can be fished effectively from shore. One of these is inlet creeks, the small, sometimes intermittently running streams that feed the pond. A stealthy approach enables us to fish both from the outside toward the creek mouth and from the creek to the pond it enters. If there is visible moving water, pass it up. Fish the still sides of it, especially if cover, like brush, cattails, willows, and sub-aquatic vegetation exist. Be very careful with each cast not to hook the cover and disturb the fish in the process of extricating the fly.

Riprap and earthen dams also provide good cover for bluegills under some conditions. Care should be taken in selection of the casting position to allow fishing in two directions along the dam from the same spot. Keep in mind that most of the productive casts are likely to be parallel to the dam and that often the corners of the dam will produce some good fish.

Deadfalls are also easily fished from shore. These bluegill magnets should be fished carefully from either side and the fan casting technique should focus on the deepest areas before casting into the shallows where fish are more wary. Sometimes would-be fishermen stand on the trunk of a downed tree while attempting to cast into the deep branches. Invariably they remark that they don't understand the poor fishing because fish should be there. The fish probably were there, of course, before having their scales scared off by noises nearly as frightening as the fall of the tree.

The most difficult structure for the landlocked fly-caster to fish is a weed bank. Only if it has a "back edge" will it be productive for wet flies. The back edge of a weed bank is the part of a pond or lake between the weed bank and the shore. This water may be several feet wide or only a few inches in width. Wet flies work well in the pockets of the back edge, which are indentations in the weed line. Surface flies and floater/diver flies can be productive if casts can be made to the outside pockets in the weeds. The outside pockets are the indentations in the weed line near the open water.

If the angler attempts to drop a weighted fly down the outside edge from shore it must result in dragging the fly back into the weeds. This is not only unproductive but alarming to the fish for several yards in either direction.

Despite some of the water being outside of casting range, bank fishing can be an extremely pleasurable and productive method. Because it is practiced by so many, it probably has accounted for more bluegills than all other methods of presentation combined.

Wading

A second effective presentation method involves wading, with or without waders. Wading should be undertaken with the strictest care, especially in older, heavily silted ponds. There are two reasons for using caution: The safety of the fisherman and the potential for harm to the aquatic environment.

The thick mud basin of most good ponds can trap a wading angler. When this occurs away from shore by even a short distance, it can be a serious problem. On more than one occasion we have had to remove our waders and step free of them before we could extricate our boots. Many times we relied on each other to help, but one especially enticing fish-producing location entrapped both of us at the same time. It was a foolishly dangerous situation that we've taken great care not to repeat.

If only one angler entered the shallows and waded completely around the pond, the plant life and spawning beds would suffer. In addition, the next angler will find a muddy trail of disturbed silt and no fish. It's an inconsiderate and short-sighted venture.

Despite these problems, we've caught many good fish, enjoyed countless hours of bluegill fly-rodding while standing waist-deep in ponds, and we heartily recommend it. Wading enables the fly-fisher backcasting room that otherwise may be nonexistent. If care is taken to choose a point of entry that allows casting to a large, productive area without moving in either direction, the impact on the environment is minimized.

The same areas previously described for the bank fisherman can be fished by the wading fly-fisher. Ponds stained enough to prevent deep weed growth may allow the wader to stand at the edge of the weeds and cast along the outside edge of the weed bank in either direction.

Waders have the added advantage of presenting a very low profile that is more difficult for the fish to see. By contrast, bank fishermen stand above the water and are much more easily spotted by the fish. To compensate for being partially submerged it is advantageous to fish a longer rod which keeps the line higher and consequently out of trouble on the back cast. When wade-fishing with a shorter rod, be aware of this lower position and throw a higher backcast than normal.

Float Tubing

Perhaps the most delightful method of presentation is float tubing. Gliding about favored waters immersed in your element in comfort and style is a delicious experience. The virtues of the ease of accessibility are unequaled. In a backpack the size of a wader bag, a fly-fisherman can carry the float tube, canvas cover, and foot pump. This means every inch of places devoid of boats, motors, and other fishermen, can be probed as long as you are willing to endure the hike. Be sure to fill the storage pockets of the canvas cover and vest with everything needed and these trips can be the highlight of the season.

The only negative aspect of float tubing involves that scourge of the pond—mud. Even floatable flippers can become hopelessly stuck in gooey mud. Velcro straps, designed to prevent losing a detached flipper, are no guarantee that the owner won't be left wallowing around like a one-legged hippopotamus. Scout the area for the best point of entry, but remember that getting in the water is the easier half of the dilemma. Shallow coves are generally poor launching points, along with any location near a feeder stream. The dam area may offer the best opportunity, but locations where trees grow near the edge of the water will likely have a firmer bottom as well. If the pond has no area solid enough to allow safe entry and exit, find the shore that drops into knee-deep or waist-deep water and try attaching a rope that will support your body weight to a nearby solid object such as a tree, sturdy bush, fence post, or your vehicle. Leave the rope dangling into the water so it can be grabbed for leverage when it's time to go home. If a safe entry and an equally uneventful exit seem unlikely, find another pond for float tubing.

Float tubing seems made-to-order for slow-moving streams. If the stream has pools too deep to wade through, try float tubing without flippers. Simply wade along until the bottom is out of reach, then go with the flow while kicking your feet to retain control. Again, the float-tuber is able to reach water that bank-bound anglers can't, while thoroughly fishing pockets of slack water left undisturbed by canoes and other larger watercraft.

Keep in mind that heavy nylon and canvas isn't armor. Avoid sharp rocks and check the tube after each trip for any unusual scrape or abrasion. By leaving a fishing partner's vehicle at the predetermined take-out point, the very long walk back to the car may be avoided.

Float tubing is great low-impact exercise. For the over-forty anglers with aching backs and knees that complain mightily about a day of walking the bank, the float tube is a painless and beneficial means of reaching good fishing water.

Float tubers, must, according to law, wear a life vest, and they should be very careful of hypothermia when tubing cold water in the early spring or late fall. Symptoms of hypothermia may not be as noticeable when the victim is submerged in water while exercising. One such incident convinced us to take occasional breaks on land and be alert for signs of lowered body temperature.

The creation of the float tube has enhanced and expanded the world of the bluegill fly-fisher, and we enjoy our float tubing adventures well into autumn.

Boats

Fishermen of all types have a wider selection of boats available to them now than ever before. Isn't it ironic that the most coveted boat style is called a bass boat? With its exceptionally stable casting platform, it must have been designed by a fly-fisher. Every high-tech gadget that has been incorporated into the design of these big lake monsters is as useful to the fly rod-wielding bluegill chaser as the ardent basser. While fly-fishermen have traditionally avoided big lakes in favor of pristine mountain streams, that choice is no longer viable for all. Those who shun the major reservoirs are the poorer for having done so. Choosing the right boat for this assignment, however, is difficult as there are many possibilities. The right boat must fit your style and needs and be adaptable to the different waters you intend to fish. Large, heavy fiberglass boats will be very stable even in windblown situations, but maneuverability, economy of initial price, and gasoline consumption will suffer accordingly. The big rigs also require more horsepower to achieve the same speed. If your lakes are very large, it's important to have enough motor to get off the lake to safety when a storm surprises you.

One of our favorite boats for fly fishing belongs to a resort owner on Kentucky Lake. It started out as an aluminum sixteen-foot bass boat but the owner had the seats removed and boat carpet laid over everything except the small steering console. Even the back deck was modified so its front edge could serve as seating while the boat was in motion. The result is a boat completely devoid of any obstruction capable of catching a loose coil of fly line. It's masterful in its simplicity, and proof that boats need not be fancy or expensive to be highly functional. Boats can also be an important part of fishing equipment in other forms. Pontoon boats are extremely popular and they can be functional as long as there is backcasting room. They provide a stable casting platform but the boat's ability to negotiate shallow water is limited and maneuverability suffers as well.

Small crafts can be perfect for lakes with fewer surface acres. Larger, heavier, wide-bodied jon boats are easily customized to be fly-fisher friendly. Carpeted half-inch marine plywood screwed into the floor ribs can provide a stable platform that will serve the standing fly-caster very well. Similarly, car-top boats are perfect for reaching those waters without launching ramps and may also work well for

Car-top boats provide easy access and great casting locations in waters that receive little fishing pressure.

floating streams where they can be dragged across gravel bars or mud flats. Canoes also provide the gentle fly-caster with access to good water. Lacking the stability of heavier, wider crafts, they nonetheless have the advantage of allowing the angler to portage into otherwise inaccessible water and are cherished by many as part of the classic fly-fishing experience.

Molded plastic boats, usually designed with two seats, are not well-suited for two fly-fishers. The seats are too closely aligned to allow safe casting. Those that are built to accommodate single anglers, however, provide yet another method of presenting flies to the bluegill population on ponds and small lakes where wind is not a problem. Kick boats fall into much the same category. Propelled by fins like a float tube, the angler is seated on a sturdy platform that can accommodate a small motor and locator. For those who feel vulnerable in a float tube, kick boats provide a wonderful alternative. Like all small craft, however, they are not safe on large lakes, rivers, and impoundments, where wind and waves may toss them around. In choosing the methods of presentation most suitable to your situation, examine the waters you regularly fish. Care in selection is the key to your satisfaction.

Delivering Your Line

After matching the method of the presentation to the situation, we need to focus on the delivery system needed to approach the fish most efficiently. The choice of the correct delivery system depends on the location of the fish to a large extent. Whether using one of the variety of watercraft, wading, or bank fishing, it's usually necessary to perform a stationary cast. Bank-fishers and waders are confined to that delivery system.

While the process of fly casting from a stationary position is infinitely pleasurable, it is not our only choice. In any of the crafts it is possible for us to drift-fish. Using the wind for propulsion, we can either continue casting conventionally or we can drag the flies through the fish. It is a silent and uncomplicated delivery system that can be modified slightly with a controlled drift presentation. Using either foot propulsion in a float tube or an electric trolling motor, it is possible to use the wind in the pre-described manner while occasionally adjusting the direction of the drift. Re-positioning will keep your fly in the fish zone longer and allow you to use this delivery even when the wind is not completely cooperative.

Trolling can also be an effective delivery system for the fly-fisher. Trolling with a fly rod has a long and storied history. Maine guides in the early twentieth century trolled streamers and "lake flies" for brook trout and landlocked salmon. Our favored species is just as worthy of the tactic and it is equally effective. Ultra slow speeds with frequent pauses to allow the fly to sink back into the fish zone is a solid presentation.

Another option is back-trolling. This tactic must be performed from a boat with a stern-mounted trolling motor. From that position, the troller has precise boat control and is able to stay "on" the weedline or brush pile being fished. Back-trolling is even more effective when the boat is being backed into a slight breeze as the depth of the presentation can be more precisely controlled.

The purpose of the delivery system is to present our flies to the bluegills in an enticing manner. To do this, several factors must be taken into account. First, we must be able to control the depth of our fly. If the fish are located in the uppermost five feet of water, the tackle need not be very complex. Floating fly line and a tapered leader that can deliver flies from a stationary casting position will

BACK-TROLLING

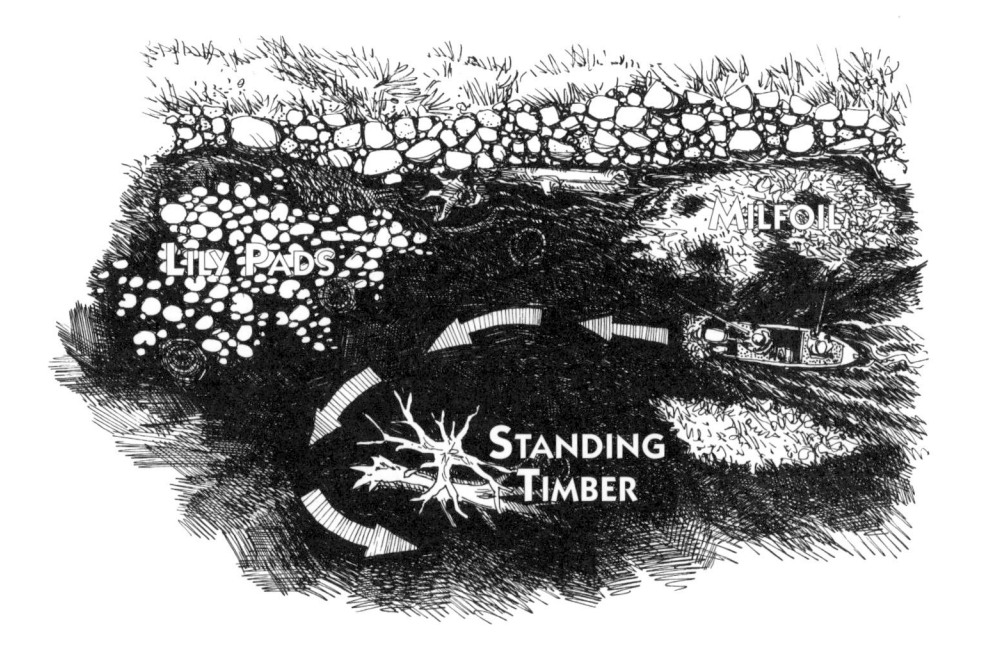

Illustration showing a boat navigating among Lily Pads, Milfoil, and Standing Timber.

suffice, but if the fish are located in from five to twelve feet of water, you need to be able to get your fly to them quickly. It's possible, of course, to simply lengthen your leader and wait while your fly sinks, but fly casting without a rod is possible too—it's just not the most desirable way to get the job done. A sink-tip line efficiently allows you to cast conventionally to these fish and deliver your fly effectively.

Several casting adjustments must be made with sink-tip line. First, don't try to pick up too much line to initiate the cast. Remember, some of it is submerged and has the pressure of the water holding it back. Also because the sinking section is heavier than the remainder of the line, the timing of the cast is different. It will be necessary to wait slightly longer on the backcast. A little practice with this specialized line, however, will enable you to make the transition smoothly.

Fish in water from twelve to twenty-five or more feet deep should be approached with a full-sinking line. Again, line-pickup and casting timing is affected by the increase in line weight. In the case of sink tip and full-sinking lines, a relatively short leader should be used so that the fly won't bow back toward the surface, thereby nullifying the use of sinking line. In all cases where depth control is necessary, whether it's one foot or twenty-five, use the countdown method described on page 93.

The disadvantages of carrying floating, sink-tip, and fast-sinking lines, especially if several different rod sizes are involved, is that they require lots of storage room. In addition, they represent a sizable expense.

A simple and inexpensive solution to the problem is a system of interchangeable front sections of varying weight densities. These are interconnected with level "running line" by a loop. The longer and heavier the added section, the deeper the fly is presented.

Another alternative is a weighted, braided leader section. These can be purchased in a variety of specific sink-rates and have the added advantages of compatibility with very light rods. Because their weight is tapered and their composition strong but flexible, they turn over small flies very nicely.

By controlling the depth of the fly, we can place it where we find the fish or at least where we feel they should be located, but unless we control the speed of the fly we won't interest many of them.

Since bluegills approach most food from behind and nearly always pause to evaluate the morsel, it is critically important, especially for selective summer fish, that the fly behave like natural food. Most of the time this means slow. This aspect of presentation can be accomplished with any of the methods we've described, but since we've already discussed trolling speeds, drifting, controlled drifts, and back-trolling, we'll focus on two practical retrieves for the stationary caster.

Stripping the Line

The easiest and most adaptable retrieve for the fly-fisher is "stripping." By pinning the line against the rod with the index finger of your rod hand, line can be pulled toward you with the line hand. One can pull or "strip" line two inches or a foot or more at a time. The retrieve can be enticing twitches accompanied by lengthy pauses or long, smooth, and rather continual. The advantage of this retrieve is its simplicity and adaptability. Its disadvantage is that it leaves looping coils of line at your feet or in the bottom of the boat.

Hand-twist Retrieve

The other practical method of working the fly is the hand-twist retrieve, which is accomplished by laying the line hand palm down along the top of the line several inches in front of the reel. Hold the line between the thumb and forefinger. By rotating or twisting the hand until the palm faces up, it will create a loop which can now be grasped by the thumb and forefinger. Repeating the process will leave the line neatly coiled in your line hand and cause the fly to react with an enticing rocking motion. This can be done either slowly or quite rapidly.

While either retrieve is effective and a matter of personal preference, it is of paramount importance that the fly be allowed to settle back to its original depth after each "pull." Both retrieves should be executed with the rod tip held low to the water, this enables the angler to easily remove all slack line and will provide a more direct connection between the rod and fish. The resulting hook-set, consequently, will be greatly enhanced.

Speed control alone can be the ingredient which causes the bluegill to take the fly, but there are many other factors capable of triggering the fish's positive response. The fly's movement or action is sometimes the critical factor in whether our offering is hit or ignored.

The fly's action can be built into the fly, imparted by the angler, or both. Any fly that has a moveable part we would describe as having built-in action. Rubber hackle, marabou, and rabbit hair are examples of material that give any fly movement when it is dropped into water or pulled through it. Others are constructed to create their own action such as jointed flies, or those with lips or collars designed to make them dive and wiggle.

From the fisherman's perspective, it may seem that the more action a fly has, the more attractive it will be to the fish. In some species, this is often true. While a largemouth bass is attracted to the commotion of a young bird falling from its nest into the water, that level of activity would scare the scales off a bluegill. Subtle action, then, is the key to attracting bluegills most of the time.

Any fly which lacks this built-in action must rely on the manipulation of the angler to impart it. This is done primarily by utilizing the stripping or hand-twist retrieve. In either case, the fly-fisher is best advised to envision the movement of the natural

Short, accurate casts to small, shaded areas can be the key to catching big bluegills.

organism being recreated. Even in the case of small minnows, the quick, darting movements are gentle as opposed to dramatic.

There are times that call for no action at all. Just the very slow fall of the imitation provides the key trigger that induces otherwise reticent bluegills into hitting.

Despite our recommendation toward slow and subtle action, there are times when more is clearly better. While these are exceptions rather than the rule, all experienced bluegill enthusiasts can recall an evening when nothing would produce but a large puffy dry fly dragged or skated across the surface, a vigorously chugged popper, or continually stripped wet pattern. These experiences dictate that we remain open-minded, experiment frequently, and above all let the bluegills tell us what action they prefer. Those who insist on using a favored fly or retrieve limit themselves to being successful far less frequently.

Another key trigger is color. Perhaps no other aspect of the fishing puzzle causes more disagreement among anglers. Everyone, it seems, has a favorite or a system of color selections they rely upon. Far too many limit their selections and, again, their own effectiveness. It's an easy trap to fall into and we've all been victimized by it. If we've had a great trip using an olive-colored fly, the next time out we may stay with olive far too long because we believe it is the bluegill's preference.

We believe that bluegills are not particularly color-selective but rather many factors combine to make some hues more visible to the fish than others. These factors relate mostly to water clarity and subsequent light penetration, conditions that are in a constant state of change. Generally, then, we choose light colors, such as white or yellow, and bright colors, like fluorescent chartreuse, when the water is clear and sunlight is plentiful, and dark colors in stained water or when the sky is heavily overcast. We believe that the dark color creates a sharp silhouette which is most easily visible to the fish under low-light conditions.

A close study of our fishing diary taken over a thirty-year period (as of this writing) indicates that our best success has come using a color progression from very light to dark as the water warms from fifty to eighty degrees or higher. The spectrum was then reversed until the water was very cool again. This pattern is consistent with our theory of color selection based on light penetration, particularly in fertile water. Colder water is heaviest and consequently suspended material less a factor. Rising temperatures reduce visibility because of the increased amount of these suspended particles.

Even these well-tested theories of color selection should not be mistaken for rules carved in stone. Once again, we should defer to the bluegills, viewing each trip as a separate entity and changing colors until they tell us what color they either prefer or can see best under conditions at that particular time.

It was precisely that attitude which led us to fish experimentally and eventually adopt an unusual color called hot pink or fluorescent red. In the past three years, our records indicate that it has been our most successful color in more different types of water and under more varied light conditions. Again, we feel it's because this color is so highly visible. As traditionalists who tended to favor natural shades like olives and browns, the use of hot pink was not an easy step to take.

While we're skeptical concerning color selectivity there is little doubt that bluegills can be frustratingly choosy regarding the size of their food. Mouth size, of course, does place restrictions on what is available to the bluegill. Bass anglers sometimes accidentally hook bluegills on bait so large it seems preposterous that the fish would consider attacking it. Yet, this inadvertent catch is more significant in explaining the bluegill's audacity than as a recommendation for fly-size selection.

The pragmatic bluegill enthusiast is likely to limit hook sizes to 6 and smaller. Unlike ambush predators like largemouth bass that may consume a large salamander and not eat again for several days, the bluegill's search for food is much more constant. Fisheries biologist and bluegill researcher, Mike Kruse, of Columbia, Missouri, explains it best, "A bluegill's mouth size forces him to feed on relatively small life forms and consequently to feed actively most of the time. Whereas a big bass may only be vulnerable to fishermen for short periods of time, big bluegill are catchable most of the time." As big bluegill enthusiasts, that's very reassuring.

Yet size selectivity isn't limited to whatever fits in the bluegill's mouth or whatever it is courageous enough to attack. There are many times when having the right pattern, color, action, speed, and depth control without exactly the right size of fly brings complete rejection. We can speculate about why this is so and generalize concerning some observations, but this is one area in which correct answers could only be provided by the bluegills. Logically, it relates to the most abundant size of its natural food source. The fish may become so focused on that size that others are disregarded. When trout become size selective, we can often observe the size of the hatch and become successful by matching it with a similar pattern and size. Of course, in still water this is much less discernible. Many times we have been successful in finding the size on which the bluegills are feeding but catch fish on a pattern and color radically different from the naturals. We have no doubt that this phenomenon is true, yet the reasons for it remain a mystery.

In our experience, bluegills become most size-conscious in the late summer when water temperatures are highest. Most of the time, we can continue to take good fish by dropping down one hook size from previous successes, but occasionally at this time a more radical downsizing is necessary. This smaller-size selectivity relates to both dry and wet patterns alike and seems not to relate to color or any other triggering mechanism.

Another potential trigger is scent or, perhaps more appropriately, taste. Five years of extensive experimentation and observation in utilizing commercially manufactured scents leaves little doubt in our minds that bluegills have the ability to smell or taste the water in evaluating a prospective meal. The manufacturers advertise these products using the testimonials of tournament fishermen and fishing's television personalities. They all attempt to convince us that their lethal effectiveness is fool-proof in beckoning fish from all corners of the lake. These claims are widely exaggerated.

We have observed bluegills moving to an unseen fly dipped liberally in commercial fish scent for a distance of no more than two feet. While this did not occur all of the time nor even the majority of the time, it was observed on a significant number of occasions. We concluded that on those occasions scent had provided the independent motivation or trigger for the strike. On many other occasions, however, it may well have provided the final inducement for an otherwise reluctant fish to take the fly. In addition, we strongly suspect that scent applied to flies causes bluegills to hold onto the fly longer, thus enabling a more positive hook-set. This alone warrants that more fly-fishermen consider the use of scent.

We found little difference in comparing one commercial product to another, but having experimented with spray-ons, liquids, gels, and even glow-in-the-dark pastes, we concluded that the material used to soak up the scent was critically important. Chenille and yarn are superior to the others we've tried.

All this discussion about what must be regarded as nothing more than "stink bait" will offend the purist nature in most of us. In our research for an article, "Is Scent Cricket?" for *Fly Fishing Quarterly* (Vol. 2 No. 1, Spring 1994, Aqua-Field Publishing Co., Inc.), we asked a cross section of notable fly-fishers from across the United States about the ethics of scent use. To no one's surprise, the answers ranged from total acceptance to cries of righteous indignation. Interestingly, the results were rigidly divided. Those who considered themselves primarily warm-water fly-fishers accepted its use, while the cold-water segment of our brotherhood couldn't bear the thought. Since ours is a gentle sport designed for our pure pleasure, it would seem reasonable that each of us resolve this issue to our own satisfaction.

Three other fly characteristics seem worthy of consideration as triggers despite the difficulty of isolating and evaluating the importance of each individually to the bluegill. Shape, texture, and sound likely play a role in the fish's final acceptance of our flies.

Fly shape receives major consideration in the construction of three flies that we use extensively. It would seem reasonable that bluegills recognize crayfish, minnows, and nymphs primarily by shape and that this recognition would be paramount in determining whether or not the fly is taken. Yet, if flies of another shape are fished in a manner that represents crayfish, minnows, or nymphs, we have no assurance that they won't receive the same attention from bluegills.

Regarding texture, it again seems reasonable that it may cause the fish to hold the fly a bit longer and therefore enhance the fish-hooking process but, clearly, evidence is lacking to support it.

One area in which we have experimented extensively is in adding sound to the fly. Water is an outstanding conductor of sound, and of course any object which moves through the water produces sound. Logically, it would follow that bluegills use their ability to detect these movements in locating food. Twelve seasons ago (at this writing), we began fishing with flies that were constructed by lashing rattle chambers to the hook shank. These little plastic or glass cylinders contained tiny beads which rattled when movement was imparted. Early in the experimental process, we determined that a sound chamber attached to a bare hook alone wasn't attractive enough to catch many fish. Our conclusion was that sound by itself was not advantageous. Similar flies, one of which had added sound, were fished side by side and produced mixed results. Sometimes the sound-enhanced fly caught more bluegills and sometimes not. The results of our testing were inconclusive. We do believe, however, that rattle-chambered crayfish flies are more effective most of the time. The rattling sound may imitate a clicking noise made by live crayfish. In our experiments, we discovered that rattle chambers made of glass produce a more audible clicking sound and found them to be more desirable. Rattle chambers may be purchased from local fly shops and mail-order companies who offer materials for warm-water flies.

Chapter 10
PUTTING THE PIECES TOGETHER

"WHY DO PEOPLE HANG TROPHY TROUT, BASS AND MUSKIES INSTEAD OF TROPHY BLUEGILLS ON THEIR DEN WALLS? BECAUSE TROPHY TROUT, BASS AND MUSKIES ARE EASIER TO CATCH THAN TROPHY BLUEGILLS!"

Chuck Tryon
Author and lecturer
1996, Rolla, Missouri

Putting It All Together

Putting together the pieces of the fishing puzzle properly means we can catch more and larger bluegills more often. Each trip to a lake, pond, or stream is a test which presents new variables requiring analysis and an appropriate response. Successful trips confirm that we have read the conditions correctly and chosen the right location, fly, and presentation. As complete bluegill fly-fishers, we want to repeat good results in a wide variety of circumstances.

The Fishing Diary

Keeping a journal of bluegill fishing trips will enable you to see the results of your puzzle-solving. Be sure to record the date, accurate weather data, and water conditions as well as the quantity and size of your catch. Include information about fly patterns you tried with hook size, color, and other ingredients such as added weight. Write a detailed description of the positioning and presentations used and be careful to note the unsuccessful methods as well as those that produced fish.

Reviewing these records at the end of the year will help in planning the next. In analyzing the year, it's helpful to break down each season and each month to understand the changes that were made to remain successful.

We've kept a bluegill diary for nearly thirty years and learn from it every season. We're still experimenting and modifying our approach to various situations but we most often use the information to duplicate previous successes under the existing conditions.

Spring Solutions

First, let's examine the easiest of all bluegill fishing situations: The spawn. A check of the water temperature in three feet of water reveals sixty-seven degrees. The small pond we're fishing is one-hundred-fifty yards long and forty yards wide. Willows line the shallow end where a tiny stream seasonally, and during heavy rains, drains a grassy pasture. Further uphill, a field is alternately planted in corn or soybeans. The earthen dam holds water to a maximum depth of fifteen feet. There is ample shallow water in the upper end and along the entire shoreline extending approximately twelve feet to a graduated depth of three feet. Several areas have emergent vegetation in the form of cattails. The water is dingy with suspended nutrients. There are two-and-a-half hours of daylight remaining of a mostly sunny 75-degree afternoon. A visual inspection reveals clusters of lighter-bottomed patches indicating the nesting process has begun. The conditions are perfect to catch lots of good-sized bluegills. What equipment and presentation might ensure the best and most enjoyable fishing?

On that occasion we assembled three-weight outfits with floating line expecting the bluegills to be shallow and knowing we could fight them in open water away from snags and brush. We decided to fish in tandem from the shore facing into the sun so as not to cast long shadows across the wary fish. We used seven-and-a-half-foot leaders tapered to 3X tippets and began by attaching a yellow Bully's Bluegill Spider in size 10. We witnessed several lusty rises so we both switched to black sponge spiders with white rubber legs tied on size 10 hooks. The action remained hot. We were careful to release the orange-breasted males behind us as we progressed around the pond. Bullfrogs serenaded us as we disassembled our rods. We had each caught and released fifty, mostly male, bluegills between eight and nine inches.

Before leaving the relative ease of the spawn, let's visit a sprawling but picturesque reservoir of 9,000 surface acres. This beautiful lake is clear and its timbered, irregular shoreline is mostly steep-sided and very rocky. The lake's excellent-fishing reputation stems from stringers of slab crappie, muskies, and better-than-average largemouth bass fishing. The bluegill fishery gets little pressure. It's early June in the lower Midwest, and seventy-degree water and eighty-five degree air has the lake full of sailboats, speed boats, and jet skiers as well as fishermen. Two large streams with many smaller tributaries join to form the irregular bottom. Standing timber was left uncut when the rock-protected concrete dam was created. Very little vegetation exists and moderate lakeshore building provides numerous docks. Intensively managed, there are a number of brush piles in twelve to fifteen feet of water and an abundance of natural structure. There's a crowd at the launching ramp and it's nearly eleven a.m. by the time we get to the water. This is a little tougher situation than our small, fertile farm pond.

We still chose three- and five-weight rods and the same Bully's Bluegill Spiders to start the trip. Checking a topographic map, we selected five very small secondary coves (coves found in larger coves). Each was checked visually before fishing. We were looking for shallow back ends of these tiny coves with either clay, sand, or gravel bottoms. We found relatively small amounts of gently sloping shorelines but those few were precious finds as the pock-marked underwater terrain was packed with aggressive fish. The tiny coves protected us from the wave action of other lake users and we had the bluegill population to ourselves. We were careful to cast to the edges of the spawning colonies first before working into the main concentration of fish. On this occasion, most hits came after the first quick, darting strip of the fly line. We left the lake at six p.m. when each of us had caught a hundred fish. Mostly, they ranged from eight to nine inches, with a few at ten inches.

Summer Problem-solving

Next, let's examine a fertile thirty-acre pond in a wooded setting. While the pond is well-protected by a hardwood forest and heavy grasses in the rather steep ravines, the watershed drains fields of grain. The maximum depth is forty-two feet in front of a rip-rap-faced earthen dam. It's mid-summer and, although overcast, still quite warm, with afternoon highs expected in the nineties. The little lake has a fairly steep-sided bank with most of the shallows located at the backs of long cove arms. Heavy moss growth drapes dock pilings and abundant deadfalls to a depth of eight feet. A healthy mid-size largemouth bass population is protected by absentee landowners who employ a caretaker. The bluegill population is large in both numbers and size. We've arrived mid-morning and will be unable to fish into the evening. How can the heat and sunlight penetration be overcome to make a successful trip?

We chose to use seven-weight rods with sink-tip line, short, four-foot leaders with a 0X tippet and a dropper rig. We felt the bluegills would be lying in the branches of the deadfalls that line either bank of the longest cove. Partly to remain cool, we utilized float tubes and positioned ourselves facing the outsides of deadfalls that extended into five to ten feet of water. We started with a Woolly Worm and a Bully's Bluegill Spider on each rod and alternated colors until the fish indicated a preference. When we recognized that most fish were being taken on smaller, dark-colored Bullys, we removed the Woolly Worm and dropped down to size 12 olive spiders. By our prearranged three p.m. departure, we had caught and released fifty-two bluegills. Most were eight inches but one specimen was a season's best at eleven inches.

Next, we'll investigate an oxbow, a backwater lake off a major river. They are created when the river channel changes course.

Selectively targeting big bluegills requires fitting the pieces of the fishing puzzle together correctly.

Heavy siltation closed the ends which once connected it to the river. Each spring the upstream snow melt and rains within the watershed cause the river's flood waters to invade the fifteen-hundred-acre lake. Many decades of these floods have caused the once sandy lake bottom to become coated with a thick layer of mud. The maximum depth is eight feet, but much of this fertile water is more shallow. Thick vines entangle the willow-encased shore and occasional areas of bulrushes dot the shallows. The water resembles a cup of strong coffee as siltation is constantly disturbed by wind and wave action and an abundant population of catfish and carp. A small rock dam sealed with silt connects the oxbow to the river by a long creek-like channel locally called a chute. The August heat would be oppressive in this humid bottom wetland, except a steady fifteen mile-per-hour north wind carries news of an impending storm. Partial cloud cover seems destined to increase. It's eight a.m. The air temperature is already eighty-two and the water is even warmer with a reading of eighty-six degrees at three feet. What are your suggestions for this unusual situation?

We decided to launch our jon boat. It's relatively heavy, with a plywood floor and extra width making it a stable craft capable of handling the wind. We both chose a seven-weight rod with sink-tip line, short leaders, and due to the low visibility in the water, heavy tippets. We selected size-8 flies ranging from crayfish patterns to small flashy streamers and launched the boat into the stiff breeze. Heading for the northernmost wind-swept bay, we positioned the boat at a right angle to the wind so it would be blown in a southerly direction. We cast our heavily weighted flies directly into the wind and drifted along without imparting much action. Occasional bursts from the trolling motor kept us on course. When we drifted from the large cove we simply reeled in our lines and motored back to the head of the lake. The wind speed was perfect to cause our flies to be dragged along near the bottom. As we lifted, then lowered our rod tips, the fly would appear to swim toward the surface then dive enticingly toward bottom. On this occasion, streamers were the bluegill's choice and our diary shows that sixty-eight were fooled by these tactics before we went home for lunch.

Skunked

All fishermen have days when they are forced to wonder about the sudden disappearance of the fish. After all, we can only make educated guesses as to their whereabouts and what may cause them to strike. Our diary reveals our fair share of embarrassing moments.

Here's a sample: In late June, several days of cloud cover had big bluegills in our favorite thirty-seven-acre pond feeding in two shallow coves. The main body of water was rimmed with coontail, and under normal conditions the face of those weed beds would provide the summertime action. Fishing had been red hot for the entire week and we placed a phone call to a friend who lived six hours away to encourage him to come and share the wonderful action. The following day, the sky was clear as the proverbial bell. The cove-feeding bluegills were nowhere to be found. We didn't think this caused much of a problem at first. We'd fish the face of the coontail, and at least provide our guest with the normally good fishing the pond provided. Wrong! Two days of intensive casting from daylight until dark produced a total catch of seven fish. We fished the coontail. We fished the rip-rap dam and even trolled the mid-lake depths. The fish had simply vanished. Had they fed so voraciously in the previous days that they saw our offerings and rejected them? Were they imbedded in the thickest part of the coontail pouting because of the weather change? Had they made a sudden change in diet and we weren't offering the right imitations? We have no idea. We do know that within twenty-four hours of our friend's departure, the bluegills began feeding normally at the edge of the weed beds. Needless to say, we didn't bother calling him to report the improvement.

On another occasion, we drove to a favored small farm pond to fish and photograph the brightly-colored bluegills we'd taken from shallow nests the evening before. The previous night had produced clear skies and much chillier temperatures followed by a brisk day. The water temperature had fallen only three degrees but obviously this was enough to drive the spawners to deeper water. We've had this happen many times and while it caused us to alter our plan, it didn't reduce the fishing as dramatically as it did on this occasion. Usually in these situations, you can fish the first break line, deeper weeds, or deep wood structure and salvage the trip. Not this time. Despite catching sixty fish the evening before, we couldn't raise a fish between us. It seemed at the time that the ones we had been catching were holding instruction seminars somewhere near the bottom and explaining to every fish how to avoid our tactics. What had happened? We can only speculate.

Don't be discouraged when these fishless trips happen. Your increased knowledge will keep them to a minimum and you will begin to figure out your share of the difficult conditions. Just as the poor outings are discouraging, discovering a productive pattern on a tough lake or under difficult circumstances is as cool as the other side of the pillow on a hot night.

Summer Streams

Before abandoning the summer period, let's visit a small gravel-studded stream that meanders through a forested valley and drains grassy pasture land and plowed fields. Seldom larger than thirty-five to forty feet across, it is a series of bubbling riffles and slow pools. While providing a summertime swimming hole for family outings and the occasional canoe floater in high water, it's usually a tranquil setting canopied by large cottonwood and sycamore trees. Numerous smallmouth and largemouth bass inhabit the river in addition to green and longear sunfish. Bluegills are abundant here, too, but rarely are the fish larger than seven and a half inches in length. They tend to be leader-shy and dash for cover when confronted with a noisy approach or sloppy cast. The weather has been hot and exceptionally dry. With air temperatures expected to top ninety degrees, we arrive with three hours of fishing time left before darkness. How would you fish this pastoral setting?

We wet-waded the evening in shorts and felt-soled wading boots covered with neoprene gravel guards. We chose three-weight rods with floating line and nine-foot leaders tapered to 4X tippets. We cast size 12 Bullys in olive, brown, and black and Woolly Worms tied on 2XL size 10 hooks with a tiny tuft of red marabou for tails. Short, accurate casts were needed to place the flies in close proximity to the tree roots, undercut banks, and overhanging tree branches that held the most fish. An entering tributary mouth provided a refuge from the current as the little stream's flow had long since stopped. In this relatively small area we were both able to catch many aggressive bluegills that had apparently been drawn to this slack-water area. In another section of the river, an abundant growth of emergent vegetation blocked the current for a rubble-strewn area several yards wide. Once again the area was a magnet for the slack-water-loving bluegills and we caught and released many. Although we lost an accurate count in the furious action, we were able to agree at a streamside campfire that more than sixty of these wild and beautiful bluegills were spending the evening with tiny holes in the corners of their mouths.

Late Summer

A forty-acre pond that serves as the water supply reservoir for a small village is located in a treeless area and is insulated from row crops by grasslands. There are two major coves and a large main lake basin with a maximum depth of twenty-seven feet. The rock-faced dam has a ninety degree angle in its center and contains a pipeline which draws water to the treatment facility. The coves contain some emergent vegetation and a thick salad-bowl of weeds cover the shallow bottoms. Recently, the evenings have been very cool, but the days remain quite warm. The water temperature has just begun to drop and high, fluffy, white clouds obscure the sun for brief periods. Ten years ago, the lake built a reputation for producing largemouth bass in the four- to eight-pound class. Anglers eventually decimated their numbers and when they were gone, abundant, but smaller, bass took their place. As a result, the bluegill population became the primary prey of the mid-sized bass and fewer but larger bluegills resulted. We arrived mid-afternoon intending to fish until dark, but recognized immediately that a stiff breeze, changeable sunlight conditions, and drop in water temperature may make fishing tough. What's your answer to this set of problems?

Actually, we didn't solve this situation satisfactorily on our first attempt nor even the second. We felt the peekaboo sunlight might be offset to some extent by the chop on the water. We chose seven-weight outfits and rigged with seven-and-a-half-foot leaders and fished Bullys and Woolly Worms in a variety of colors and sizes off the first break line fished from shore by casting into the wind. After an hour and a half, we had but five average fish between us and decided to change tactics. Next, we launched a car-top boat and switched to reels loaded with sink-tip line and shortened leaders. Using the wind, we drifted the deeper sections and mouths of coves as well as main lake points. The results were equally poor, with only three fish taken in more than an hour. Again, a change was in order. With the sun now at a lower angle, we hoped less sunlight penetration would cause the bluegills to feed heavily in the shallows. This time we were right. Changing back to floating lines, we walked along the lengthy rip-rap dam tossing size 8 crayfish patterns into the sharp rocks ahead of us. It was like flipping a switch. Big hungry bluegills were attending a banquet. By sunset, we had each released more than thirty eight- to nine-inch fish, and one in excess of eleven. This trip demonstrates the need to keep moving and keep adapting your approach. Usually there is an answer.

Mid-Autumn

At the height of the autumn season there is a time when the leaves are at their peak of color and the sky is its richest blue. The air and water are both seventy degrees and you feel fortunate to be able to be on the water during "Indian summer." Let's visit a large multi-use impoundment with heavy growth of milfoil and many serpentine coves. Homes dot the irregular shoreline and private docks are abundant. We're several miles from the large concrete dam and lake traffic is particularly heavy as many have anticipated this to be the last chance to frolic in good weather. The main lake is steep-sided and deep but the secondary coves are shallow. We're fishing late morning through late afternoon to take advantage of the warmest temperatures of the day. Where would you look for big late-season bluegills?

We launched the boat at a main lake cove. It contained six smaller coves each lined with docks. Using seven-weight outfits and sink-tip line, we began probing various depths of each dock with size 8 Woolly Buggers and crayfish patterns as we glided along using the trolling motor. These tactics were proving successful and quite satisfactory until we heard the sucking noises made by feeding bluegills. Hundreds, perhaps even thousands, of fish were feeding heavily on the inside edge of the matted milfoil where a lengthy stretch of gravel shoreline prevented weed growth. Quickly, we switched to floating lines and small popping bugs. We weren't matching the tiny insects that were hatching there but the ravenous bluegills didn't care. Eventually, we settled on size 12 black sponge spiders, but a quiet approach and soft cast seemed to be the key. We anchored and from that one location we caught sixty-six bluegills before the action began to slow. Always remain alert to any sign that may help increase your catch.

Late Autumn

Your friends are either hunting or have retired to the tying vice. With water temperatures in the mid-forties and the air even cooler, we need to bundle up to be comfortable.

Let's examine a large impoundment of twenty-four thousand acres which is generally steep-banked with beautiful areas of rock-sided shoreline. The water is very clear and its reputation centers around smallmouth bass that grow so large it has produced a state record. A wide variety of other game fish inhabits the lake but the bluegills receive little pressure. Nearly devoid of vegetation, there are coves filled with standing timber. Lots of coves and secondary coves provide ample shallow water. Air and water temperatures are in the forties, but the normally busy lake hosts only the most die-hard anglers on this day. Where should we look for the bluegill population?

We chose a small cove full of standing timber and protected from the raw wind. We used full-sinking line on seven- and nine-weight rods and felt certain the bluegills would be suspended in the tree branches. We used a locator to help eliminate the ones that didn't hold fish. On this day, we found the fish at twenty feet near the

Tandem or dropper rigs can sometimes produce double hookups of big bluegills capable of thrilling even the most jaded angler.

outer branches of large trees located off secondary points. We dropped one-inch-long white and silver marabou streamers among them with great success. It was important to watch the line closely as it fell because the fish were inclined to hit on the drop. Any hesitation in the line got a hook-set but sometimes a branch intercepted the fly. The hang-ups had to be broken off and usually put the bluegills off, thus requiring the location of another productive tree. Five hours of midday probing produced a nice catch of thirty-two bluegills that averaged eight inches.

While it's important to learn to read the conditions and make educated guesses concerning their location and what will trigger hits, it's equally significant to learn to listen to the bluegills. Knowing how to piece together a major pattern causes us to realize how many more fish can be caught by paying attention to details. Casting accuracy, proper leader length for the situation, right-sized tippet, good line control, sharp hooks, and the right retrieve are important considerations.

Fish often. Only the most expert angler can fish once a month and still know where the fish are located and which fly they want.

Have fun.

BIBLIOGRAPHY

Chandler, Leon. *"Bluegill: Tops for Fun Fishing," The Flyfisher.* Sandpoint, ID: Keokee Publishing, Summer 1994.

Ellis, Jack. *The Sunfishes.* Bennington, VT: Abenaki Publishers, Inc., 1993.

Kreh, Lefty. *The Professionals' Favorite Flies Volume I—Dry Flies, Emergers, Nymphs & Terrestrials.* Birmingham, AL: Odysseus Editions, Inc., 1993.

Krieger, Mel. *The Essence of Fly Casting.* San Francisco, CA: Club Pacific, 1987.

Meyer, Deke. *Float Tube Fly Fishing.* Portland, OR: Frank Amato Publications, Inc., 1989.

Nemes, Sylvester. *The Soft-Hackled Fly.* Old Greenwich, CT: The Chatham Press, 1975.

Nixon, Tom. *Fly Tying and Fly Fishing for Bass and Panfish.* Cranbury, NJ: A. S. Barnes and Co., Inc., 1968.

Schwiebert, Ernest. *Nymphs.* Tulsa, OK: Winchester Press, 1973.

Schullery, Paul. *Home Waters.* Gary Soucie, Ed. New York, NY: Fireside Books, 1991.

Stewart, Dick and Farrow Allen. *Flies for Bass and Panfish.* Intervale, NH: Northland Press, 1992.

Tryon Chuck and Sharon. *Figuring Out Flies.* Rolla, MO: Ozark Mountain Flyfishers, 1990.
—*Fly Fishing for Trout in Missouri.* Rolla, MO: Ozark Mountain Flyfishers, 1985.

Whitlock, Dave. *L.L. Bean Fly Fishing for Bass Handbook.* New York, NY: Nick Lyons Books, 1988.

INDEX

Accardo, Tony 44, 96
Accardo-Peckinpaugh Company 44
Adams 45
Alabama 14
Arkansas 14-15, 48, 93
attractor pattern 43, 69, 107
back-trolling 130, 131 *illus.*, 132
backwater lakes 84, 142
bamboo 24
barbless hook 32, 98
barbell eyes 72, 110
bank fishing 125, 130
bass 68,85,105,136
  largemouth 17, 19, 37, 76, 79, 81, 85, 94, 96, 105-107, 109, 133, 136, 141-142, 145-146
  smallmouth 18-19, 67, 87, 145,148
  white 69
bayous 20, 47, 78, 86
bendback flies 110, 118
Black Ghost Marabou 69
Black Gnat 46, 97, 106
Black Nose Dace 68
bluegill factories 76
bluegill size 13-14
bluegill growth rate 14
boats 34-35, 128-130
boat, speed control 118
boat bag/tackle box 30
Borger, Gary 101
braided loop 26
breakline 99
bream 17
bream killers 47, 65
Bully's Bluegill Spider 65, 93, 97, 99, 103,

111, 114-115, 141-142, 146-147
fishing technique for 39-40
  recipe 41-42
bulrushes 79, 143
caddisflies 48, 104
Cajun Coachman 47, 103
canals 89
canoes 34, 127
Catalpa Worm 70
Caterpillar 70
Cave, Jon 104
Centrarchidae 17
chenille 38, 137
Chironomid 75, 106
chizzy-wink 104
closed-cell foam 45, 107
coal strip mine pits 88
coontail 78, 144
controlled drift 118, 130, 132
cork flies 44-45
cork poppers 44, 96
count down method 93, 132
counting down the fly 19, 28, 48, 99, 109, 119, 122
crayfish 70-72, 111, 138, 144, 147-148
"cruisers" 106
Dacron backing 25
damselflies 104
deadfalls 80, 84, 86, 124, 142
deer-hair bugs 28, 38, 44-45, 70
diary, fishing 135, 140, 144
docks 70, 80, 111,

141-142, 147-148
"dog days" 13, 107
dragonflies 104
drift fishing 84, 108-110, 118, 130, 144, 147
dropper rig
  See tandem rig
dry flies 27-28, 44-46, 85, 106-107, 114, 134
Duncan loop 26-27
Ellis, Jack 23, 47, 70, 96
emergers 30, 106
The Essence of Flycasting (Krieger) 26
eutrophication 74
fan casting 124 *illus.*, 123-124
Fathead Diver 47, 96, 104
Federation of Fly Fishers 72
feeding habits 18-19, 46, 66, 68, 71, 75, 79, 84, 88, 93-94, 96, 99-102, 104-106, 108-109, 113-114, 116, 119-120, 123, 136, 144-145, 147-148
Figuring Out Flies (Tryon) 71
Flex-light 31
float tubes, float tubing 24, 33-34, 95, 106, 108, 110, 126-127, 129-130, 142
Float Tube Fly Fishing (Meyer) 34, 91
floatant 28

floater/divers 44, 47, 125
flooded timber 84
Florida 88
flowages 20
flybox 30,35
Fly Fishing for Trout in Missouri (Tryon) 71
Fly Fishing Quarterly, 137
fly lines 23, 25-26, 33, 39, 128, 130, 142
  fast-sinking 102, 132
  floating 25-26, 122, 130, 132, 141, 146-148
  full-sinking 25, 27, 109, 120, 122, 131, 148
  sink-tip 25, 27, 92, 99, 102, 109, 131-132, 142, 144, 147
fly rods 16-17, 23-26, 28-34, 40, 103, 120, 126, 131-132, 141-142, 144, 146, 148
  bamboo 24
  graphite 24
fly shape 138
fly selection 31, 103, 114
fly size 24, 71, 104, 114, 116, 136
fly texture 138
Fly Tying and Fly Fishing for Bass and Panfish (Nixon) 36, 47
The Flyfisher 72
Foam Beetle 70
foam spider 45
forceps 32
Galyardt, Dennis 72
Galyardt's Foxy

Crayfish 72
Gill Getter 65
Gold Ribbed Hare's Ear Nymph 67, 120
green sunfish 17
Grizzly King 48, 107, 118
Halblom, David 77, 111
head cement 39, 42
Henshall bug 37
Holman, Walt 107
home waters 89-90, 109
Home Waters (Soucie, ed.) 73
hook disgorger 32
hook hone 31
hook,
  Limerick bend 103
  Mustad 94840 39, 45
  perfect-bend 103
  turned-down eye 103
hook-set 16, 32, 44, 97, 103-104, 133, 137, 149
Hudson, T. S. 14
Hum Bug 65, 97
hydrilla 79
impoundments,
  impounded lakes 20, 74, 76, 82, 89, 103, 114, 129, 147-148
inlet creeks 84-85, 124
insects, aquatic 66, 107
jointed flies 133
keel fly 110, 118
Kentucky 14
Kentucky Lake 128
Ketona Lake, Alabama 14
kick boat 129
Kreh, Lefty 43
Krieger, Mel 26
Kruse, Mike 93-94, 96, 136
Krystal Flash 69, 72, 93
L.L. Bean Fly Fishing for Bass Handbook (Whitlock) 121
lake, natural 20, 74-75, 77, 82, 89
  middle-aged 83 illus.
  older 77, 83 illus., 102-103, 125
  young 74, 83 illus-.
Lake Okeechobee, Florida 92, 104
Lepomislvlacrochirus 17, 20, 45
leader 26-28, 72, 92, 110, 122, 130-131, 141-142, 144, 146-147, 149
leader, braided 26, 132
leader sink 28
leader straightener 28
Letort Cricket 70
lily pads 79, 86
locator, fish 35, 109-110, 102, 118-119, 122, 129
longear sunfish 17, 145
Louisiana 44, 47
magnifying lenses 31
marabou 93, 116, 120, 133, 146, 149
marsh 47, 86

matching the hatch 45, 68, 104, 107, 136
mayflies 45, 66, 68, 104, 114-115
McGinty 46
Meyer, Deke 34, 91
Mickey Finn 69
micro jig 70, 72, 103, 120
midges 75, 104
milfoil 78, 147-148
minnows 68-69, 79, 96, 103, 105, 114, 134, 138, 149
Mississippi 14
Missouri 14, 66, 71, 79, 93-94
Mosquito 46, 104
moss 37, 72, 85, 99, 102, 104, 111, 142
moving water (see also streams) 34, 66,69, 72, 84, 86, 88, 124
nail knot 26
National Freshwater Fishing Hall of Fame 14-16
Nemes, Sylvester 48
Nixon, Tom 36, 47, 70
North Carolina 14
North Fork Nymph 66, 115, 120
nutrients 18, 74, 77, 84-85, 140
nymphs 30, 44, 65-66, 67-69, 97, 99, 101, 105-106,114-115, 120, 138
Nymphs (Schwiebert) 66
Oklahoma 14
oligochaetes 71
Orange Fish Hawk 48, 97
Oscar's Hexagenia Nymph 68
"other flies" 44, 70
oxbows 84, 142
oxygen depletion 78, 89
oxygen levels 79, 102
pH 88, 102
Peckinpaugh, E. H. 44
Pelican Lake, Minnesota 92
phosphate strip-pits 88
ponds 13, 15, 18, 20, 24, 32, 35, 42, 46, 66-68, 77-81, 84-85, 87, 89, 94, 100, 106, 108, 115, 119, 122-127, 129, 139-142, 144-146
poppers 28, 44-45, 85, 96, 104, 107-108, 114, 134
predators 76, 79-82, 88, 102, 106, 136
presentations 95, 108-110, 113-115, 118, 120-126, 129, 130, 132
The Professionals' Favorite Flies Volume I- Dry Flies, Emergers, Nymphs & Terrestrials (Kreh) 43
Professor 48, 107, 118

rabbit hair 133
record catches 14
map 15
redear sunfish 17
reels 25
  single-action 25
  automatic 26
  extra spool 26
  pin-on 28
renegade 46, 106
reservoirs 35, 42, 76, 82, 128, 141, 146
retrieves
  hand-twist 40, 47, 97, 133
  strip 39-40, 47, 97-98, 103, 132-134, 142
riprap 85, 124, 142, 144, 147
roll casts 24, 40, 86
rootwads 87
Round Dinny 44
rubber hackle 39, 45, 65, 133
San Juan Worm 71
"satellites" 93
scent 137
Schullery, Paul 73
Schwiebert, Ernest 66
Scud (olive) 67
sediment 74, 84
selectivity 13, 18-19, 45, 88, 100, 105-106, 111, 114-115
  color 132
  size: 135-137
shad, threadfin 69
siltation 84, 143
sliders 44
sloughs 20
"sneakers" 93
soft-hackle fly 47, 48, 97
sound, in bluegills' environment 123
sound, fly 19, 138
spawn 12-13, 18, 20, 44-45, 79-80, 86, 92-94, 96-97, 99-101, 103, 115, 125, 140-142, 145
  post-spawn 70
  pre-spawn 42, 92
sponge spiders 44-45, 107, 141, 148
Stevenson, Fred 12
stoneflies 104
Stout, Michael Robert 15
streams 20, 34, 42, 45, 48, 67, 77, 80-81, 86-90, 114-120, 122, 124, 127-129, 140-141, 143, 145-146
streamers 44, 68-69, 93, 103, 105, 111, 122, 130, 144, 149
strip-mine pits 20
structure 40, 74, 80, 86, 88, 93, 109-111, 124-125, 141, 145
submerged timber 110
sunfish 17
The Sunfishes (Ellis) 23, 101
suspended bluegill 109-

110, 118, 122, 148
swamp 86
tandem rig 116-117, 142
tape measure 32
Tellico Nymph 67, 97
Terrestrials 44, 70, 104, 107, 108, 114
The Soft Hackled Fly (Nemes) 48
Thunder Spin (white) 69
tippets 15, 27-28, 72, 110, 115-117, 120, 141-142, 144, 146, 149
topwater flies 44
tree roots 86, 146
thermometer 100
triangulation 102
trolling 89, 118, 130, 132
Tryon, Chuck 71, 77, 139
ultraviolet light 26
vegetation 24, 46, 66-67, 70, 72, 74, 76, 78-79, 81-82, 84-86, 88-89, 102-104, 110, 124, 140-141, 146, 148
vertical jigging 110, 118, 120
vest 29-30, 33
Vogele, Lou 48, 80, 93
waders 32-33, 125-126, 130
wading 95, 125-126, 130
wading accessories 33
wading shoes 32
water temperature 80, 82, 91-93, 100, 102, 109, 112-113, 115-116, 118-119, 122, 136, 140, 145-148
weed guards 47, 104, 110, 118
weighted flies 28, 92, 96, 102, 109, 120, 122, 125, 144
wet-fly patterns 44, 47, 93, 97, 114, 118, 134, 137
Whitlock, Dave 67, 121
Whitlock's Damselfly Nymph (olive) 67
Wildcat 44
Woolly Bugger 97, 99, 111, 148
Woolly Bugger (olive) 69
Woolly Worm (white) 48
Woolly Worm 97, 116, 142, 146-147
worms 70-71
worm imitations 70
Wulff, Lee 29
Yuk Bug 65, 103

INDEX 151

Treat yourself
and your angling partner . . .

...to a fly fishing and tying feast with subscriptions to **Flyfishing & Tying Journal.** You'll marvel at the helpful, colorful creativity inside this 100-plus page quarterly masterpiece of publishing!

You've worked hard, now sit back and drink in the elixir of fly-fishing potential that we provide you, featuring fine printing on top-quality paper. We are terribly excited with our generous, friendly fly-fishing publication and know you will love it also! Please share our joy of discovery and subscribe today!

Strike a deal for only $9.99 for one year.

Order a subscription below for you and your angling friend.

SUBSCRIBE HERE!

Please send me:

☐ One year of **Flyfishing & Tying Journal** for only $9.99 (4 big issues)

☐ Two years of **Flyfishing & Tying Journal** for only $19.95 (8 issues)

☐ Check enclosed (US Funds)   ☐ New   ☐ Renew

☐ Charge to:

☐ Visa ☐ MC CC#:_____ Exp: _____

(Canadian & foreign orders please add $5/year)

Phone orders: 1-800-541-9498 or 503-653-8108. FAX 503-653-2766. Call 8 to 5 M-F, Pacific Standard Time.

Name: _____

Day Phone:(_____)_____

Address: _____

City:_____ State:_____ Zip: _____

FRANK AMATO PUBLICATIONS • P.O. BOX 82112 • PORTLAND, OR 97282